Rubyville

A Place of Refuge

BOOK TWO

5-13-2017 Deborah Ann Dykeman

Melissa,
Thank you
for your support!
Deborah Ann Dykeman

ISBN: 1523943106
ISBN-13: 978-1523943104

Books in the Rubyville Series

A Place to Call Home

A Place of Refuge

A Place to Heal
(coming Summer 2016)

Also by Deborah Ann Dykeman

To Thee I'm Wed

Dedication

I dedicate this book to my four lovely daughters:
Britta Ann, Courtney Lea, Alyssa Lynn, and Catherine Emily.
I have raised them the best way I knew how, before the Lord. And yet,
they are still women with flaws, just as I am. I pray that I continue to grow
in my Christian walk and in that, I will be a testimony to each of them as
they learn to love their husbands and their children. I am so thankful
that we serve a patient and loving God who allows us so many chances to
'get it right'. And Catherine, you are the lucky one that I have the
opportunity to practice on even longer!
I love you all!
Mom

Acknowledgements

Thank you, as always, to my family. You all have been very supportive,
each of you in your own way.
Britta Ann and Alyssa Lynn, thank you for your editing skills
and going through the story just 'one more time'.
And thank you, Catherine, even though your horse
did not make it on the cover.
Thanks to our son, Nathan, for his computer help, and our son-in-law
Mitchel. You guys work so quickly that I will never be able to
understand what you do!
Thank you to our son-in-law, David, who always shares my posts
and offers a word of encouragement.
Jon and Courtney Lea, you are doing the best work of all right now,
bringing another grandchild into this world.
Thank you for your prayers and encouragement.
As always, thank you to Julia Ryan for her fantastic cover design! She has
brought this series to life for me with her talents.
I can't wait to show all of you the next two books! They are just as lovely!
And most of all, thank you, George, for being my husband and sharing this
journey with me. You are always there with a smile and
helping any way you can. You are loved!

Chapter One

St. Louis, Missouri
January 1896

"MAY I WALK YOU ladies home?" Thomas offered his arm to Annabella as he placed his top hat upon his blond head. "The air is a bit chilly, if I may say so. The companionship will help the time pass more quickly."

Annabella returned the blue-eyed gaze with her own green one and smoothed a strand of red hair from her cheek. She pulled on her kid-leather gloves and gave him a smile. "Yes, the weather has taken a definite turn for the worse. But we are just a few blocks from home. Beth and I will be just fine. It seems a shame for you to walk us home and then have to retrace your steps back to your residence."

Beth looped her arm through Annabella's. "We always have fun and talk about interesting topics when we walk."

Thomas smoothed his blond mustache around his lips and followed the length of his short beard to a point and sighed. "Well, if you are sure." He glanced up at the sky. "You have a few more minutes of daylight or I would insist on accompanying you."

Annabella gave a short laugh. "We will be fine, Mr. Pratt. You should know me well enough by now to know that I will stay safe and take *every* precaution."

Thomas cleared his throat and adjusted the velvet collar of his overcoat. His eyes met hers once more. "Well then, until next time, Miss Barton, Beth." He tipped his hat and proceeded down the sidewalk, his tall form straight and stiff.

Beth shook her head as they turned to follow the sidewalk in the opposite direction. "I do not think Mr. Pratt was very pleased with your decision."

"He seldom is. I am much too independent and opinionated."

"Is that wrong?"

Annabella sighed. "I do not think it is wrong for a woman to know what she believes and to state it. She should stand firm if the need arises, always having the utmost respect when doing so. Most men do not think that is necessary."

"I do not understand."

Annabella smiled down at the blonde head. "This is probably a conversation left until you are older."

"But I thought I *was* older."

"You are growing up quickly, Beth. But twelve is still a little young to understand some things. Right now your job is to concentrate on your school work and do the chores you are given around the house."

"Mama Bella, when do you think Mr. Pratt will ask to marry you?" Beth tossed one long braid behind her shoulder with her gloved hand. "Because I know he wants to." Beth smiled up at Annabella and gave her another saucy grin.

Annabella returned the smile and squeezed the gloved hand that she held. "Yes, you and Aunt Agnes keep informing me of Mr. Pratt's intentions, but he has yet to ask for my hand in marriage."

Beth stopped their chilly walk home and put her gloved hands on her hips. "You know that is not true! I have heard him talk of marriage with you." Beth bit her lower lip and looked down at the white ground. Her cheeks, apple-red from the cold, deepened to a darker hue.

Annabella raised a brow, her green eyes twinkling. "Have you? Then might I suggest that when you are sneaking around trying to eavesdrop, you listen very carefully." Annabella grasped Beth's hand in hers, continuing down the snow-packed walk. "Yes, Mr. Pratt has talked of marriage, but he has not formally asked."

"But don't you want him to?" Beth placed a small hand at her chest. "I just think it is *so* romantic that he wants to marry you. I would have said 'yes' *ages* ago."

"Well, we will not have to worry about that for a few years now, will we?" Annabella glanced up at the darkening sky. "It looks like it could snow again. I would like to be home, warm and cozy, before it does." She pulled the high neck of the cape about her chin and gave a small shiver.

They turned right onto Missouri Avenue, greeting the few people courageous enough to be out in the wintry, late afternoon. "I think Lafayette Square is the most beautiful place to live. What do you think?" Beth looked up at Annabella and then gestured toward Lafayette Park. "Even in January the trees are pretty."

Annabella smiled and nodded. "Yes, they are pretty, but I love the shade in the summer and the colors of the leaves in the fall."

Beth pursed her lips and frowned. "Yes, I do like them in the summer. The flowers are lovely too." Beth swung their clasped hands. "Someday, I want to see Rubyville in the winter. I have only been there in the summer. Why is that?"

Annabella laughed. "You are full of questions today! I go home in the summer because it is easier to travel then." She pointed at Beth, "You have school as well, remember?"

"I remember," Beth sighed.

"Well, that is a big reason you have not been to Rubyville during the school year. I also enjoy being out of the city for a few months when it is so hot."

"Isn't it hot in Rubyville?"

"Yes, the weather is a lot like here in St. Louis, but I guess it just feels better in the country, in my mind. When the wind blows it smells fresh and clean and I can walk beside the river where it's always shady and cool. I can ride Strawb—" Annabella gulped and took a deep breath.

"I know you are sad about your horse dying, but surely you can get another one." Beth squeezed Annabella's hand. "I will be praying that God sends another one to Rubyville for you. I think she should be white with a long, black mane and tail."

Annabella brushed at her cheek. "That sounds like a beautiful combination to me."

They turned onto the swept bricks leading to the three-story house. The arches above each window and the stately front door welcomed them as the light glowed from inside. They climbed the short flight of stone steps and stomped the snow from their boots before opening the heavy oak door.

"I am so glad you two are back. It looks like we have another storm on the way." Agnes took their capes and gloves and proceeded to the back of the house. "Your slippers should be nice and warm by the fire in the parlor. I had Arthur get them a few minutes ago."

Annabella entered the front parlor and was welcomed by a bundle of navy blue velvet. The five-year old Ruth grasped Annabella's legs and buried her chubby face in her skirt. Annabella placed her hand on the mop of brown curls and laughed. "I missed you too. Let me sit down and take off my wet boots so I can put on my slippers. My feet are freezing!"

Ruth backed away and grabbed Annabella's slippers, setting them in front of their owner. She took the smaller pair from the hearth and set them before Beth. "I'll help," she stated as she sat on the hand-carved rug and unlaced Beth's boots.

"Now where did that boy get to?" Agnes entered the room and placed two thin hands at her hips. "I thought he was here just a minute ago."

A brown head of tousled curls peeked from around the green, velvet sofa. "I'm still here. I'm just finishing another chapter before bed."

Agnes shook her head. "I have never seen a boy your age read as much as you. We will be out of books before too long and then what are you going to do?" She gave him a smile and a wink before sitting on the sofa. "Did the bread arrive nice and warm?" She glanced between Beth and Annabella. "I made sure those potatoes were right out of the oven. They should have kept everything toasty."

Annabella patted her aunt's shoulder. "It was still warm enough to melt butter. I am so glad we made extra today. With this cold weather, their little tummies need to be full."

"Well, at least they are out of the cold and they will have a blanket tonight. That is better than they have had in the past."

Arthur stood and leaned against the arched back of the sofa. "Why do people leave their children out in the cold? Don't they miss them? I miss my papa and mama...Ruthie does too." Arthur looked to his sister for affirmation. With her nod, he continued. "But our papa and mama didn't leave us on purpose. God wanted them to be with Him…right?"

Agnes placed her hand on Arthur's arm and stroked the wool material. "Sometimes parents leave their children because they do not have any other choice. They take them to a home for children so they can be cared for by people like us and Mr. Pratt. That way they can have a warm place to live with food and clothing."

"I know the home is much better than living on the streets, but I am still thankful that we can live with you. I remember living at the home, and I still miss my friends, but I would miss you both more." Beth looked between the two women seated on the sofa. "I thank God every day that I can be here and I know Arthur and Ruthie do too." Two curly heads nodded in agreement. "I am also praying that someday we can have another mother and father to love us and take care of us. I know we will not be here with you forever."

Annabella rushed to where Beth sat and pulled her into a hug. "I do not want to hear any of that kind of talk. We have known you since you were practically a baby. All three of you are part of our family until God shows us otherwise. Even then, we will always remain in contact. We would never just let you go live with someone else and not write or visit if we were able."

Beth buried her blonde head in Annabella's shoulder. "I love you so much! I never want to leave here. I want to be with you both forever."

ANNABELLA GLANCED AT THE stately grandfather clock in the corner. "It is almost nine, Aunt Agnes. I think I will head up to bed, maybe read for a bit."

Agnes placed the baby blanket she was knitting in the basket at her feet. "I think I am going to head up, too. Were you able to finish the letter to your parents?"

"Just about, I have maybe another page to go. You know how much Mama loves a long letter with lots of stories." Annabella rubbed the palm of her hand. "My fingers are a little sore anyway. I will finish it tomorrow night."

Agnes smiled and nodded her head. "Yes, Lavinia always did enjoy a bit of gossip. She would never admit to that, of course. She would say it would 'help her pray more effectively'."

Annabella laughed. "You sound as though you could be Mama's younger sister."

"Only by four years, mind you. Lavinia took great advantage of that on many occasions, when it suited her purpose."

Annabella leaned back in the chair and rested her elbow on the writing desk. "I was always telling Poppa that it seemed strange that you and Mama were sisters. You are so very different from one another."

Agnes nodded. "That is a fact. Lavinia would never have remained 'an old maid' such as I have...and then taken in children to care for, to boot."

"Do you ever regret not marrying?"

Agnes shook her head in the negative. "I have not. I love my life just as it is. I am free to help at the children's home and the church. I can go where I am needed. I would not have that freedom if I had a husband to care for. I know that is not proper for a woman, but I am content." She smiled and nodded toward Annabella. "I have a beautiful niece to help me, as well as three children needing care and love. I would say my life is just about perfect for me."

Annabella sighed and rubbed a fingernail along the grained top of the desk.

Agnes followed the movement with her eyes. "Are you happy with your life, Annabella?"

"Usually I am." Annabella sighed and rose from the chair, arching her back before joining Agnes on the tufted sofa. "Beth asked me on the way home tonight if I knew when Mr. Pratt would ask me to marry him. I know he wants to ask, but I just keep him from the topic whenever I can."

"Why is that, Annabella? Have you thought of why you avoid the issue?"

Annabella folded her hands in her lap and let her shoulders droop. "I do not know, Aunt Agnes. I have known him almost five years. We attend services at the same church; we help at the children's home and take food to the poor. He is patient and kind. He is not the handsomest of men, but I am not the most comely of women either. It would seem that we would be the perfect match."

"Do you love him?"

"I believe that is where the problem lies. He is more of a brother to me than a suitor. I enjoy being with him, talking with him, but I do not love him in the way a woman should love a man."

"Many marriages are made on less, Annabella. Maybe you would grow to love him?"

Annabella smiled at her aunt. "Now you *do* sound like Mama. She was devastated when I did not marry Orin Langworthy. She thought I would never have another chance to marry again."

"Have you told her about Mr. Pratt's intentions?"

"I have told her that a gentleman my age visits frequently and that we work together." Annabella glanced at her aunt.

Agnes laughed. "I see that look, Annabella and as we just discussed, I know your mother. She would not have been content with that information."

"You are correct. Just as soon as she found out that he was not married, she set her mind to getting *us* married. I am surprised she has not shown up here in St. Louis to make sure the goal is accomplished."

"Well, the weather has been rather nasty. But spring is coming." Agnes laughed and patted Annabella's clasped hands. "I know you are struggling with this, but only you can decide if Mr. Pratt is the right man for you. Do you still care for Mr. Langworthy?"

"I thought at first that might be the problem." Annabella gripped her hands tighter. "Mr. Langworthy was everything that Mr. Pratt is not. He was taller than me, with dark hair and a mustache. Mr. Pratt just seems to pale in comparison on all levels. I do not know if I can spend the rest of my life looking 'eye-to-eye' with my husband."

"Dear niece, you are tall for a woman. That last statement may be difficult to change." Agnes gave a short laugh. "Does it matter anyway? If you really love someone, their height or physical appearance should not be a criteria for marriage."

Annabella snorted. "I realize I can be shallow, but the outside appearance is not even the issue. I want to be married to someone that challenges me. I would like to have an intelligent conversation and not be thought of as silly because I am female."

"Does Mr. Pratt make you feel that way?"

Annabella chewed on her lower lip. "He seems over-protective and fussy to me. Again, more like a brother. I enjoy talking with him and I respect him and his viewpoint on many things." Annabella sighed heavily and looked at her aunt. "There is just no *excitement* there, no surprises."

"Mr. Langworthy was exciting and full of surprises?" Agnes rubbed her chin, her brown eyes sparkling.

Annabella laughed and playfully tapped her aunt's knee. "*Now* you are just provoking me."

"It sounds as though you keep comparing Mr. Pratt to Mr. Langworthy and poor Mr. Pratt is found lacking each and every time."

Annabella nodded.

"You have not seen Mr. Langworthy in almost ten years, Annabella. Are you building him up in your mind, making him something he never was?"

She shook her head in the negative. "I really do not think I am. He was perfect for me. We had such good times together, riding around Rubyville, discussing so many topics. He talked with me like he was really interested in what I had to say. He made me feel loved and important. My opinion mattered to him. We built a house together…a place to call home and raise a family."

"But were those things that important to him, Annabella?" Agnes asked the question with gentleness. "He sacrificed his relationship and future with you when he committed the indiscretion that he did."

"I know, and it just makes me angry every time I think about it!" Annabella clenched her fists and looked at her aunt. "I get so upset when I think of what he did that night. I can still hear them…their whispered words in the darkness. It has been so long ago, and yet it still bothers me. That cannot be alright. I should be over that whole mess by now."

"Maybe that is the reason you will not let yourself have feelings for Mr. Pratt. There could be a part of you that still loves Mr. Langworthy and another part that will not trust another man."

Annabella gave a big yawn, covering it with one hand. "I think the part that will not trust is much bigger than the other part. It is difficult to say. I never saw him after that night. It might have been better if I had spoken with him."

Agnes pushed the knitting basket to the side of the sofa and stood. "Maybe God knew that would not be the best thing to happen at the time."

"You are probably right. I was very angry. I would have said things I would have regretted."

"We all have a time or two when that happens. You are not the first and you will not be the last. What matters is how you handle it in the end." She leaned over and gave Annabella a hug. "I am headed to bed. The coals on that fire are not doing much to keep it warm in here. I will be praying for you, my dear and the decision you need to make where Mr. Pratt is concerned."

"I *need* to make a decision?" Annabella frowned and bit her bottom lip.

"Yes, you do. The poor man has to get on with his life and find someone else to share it with if you are not interested. As you said, it has been almost five years."

"I suppose you are right. I am just afraid to stir the pot."

"It has been simmering long enough. You need to either take it off the heat or put another stick of wood in the stove."

Chapter Two

"MISS BARTON, DO YOU really need to leave? I certainly have treasured this time with you. Not many people want to read from the 'good old book' anymore."

Annabella rose from the wood chair and took her cape from the back, placing it about her shoulders. She smoothed the front of her skirts. "It has been a nice time for me as well, Mrs. Cobb. I have enjoyed reading to you as much as you have enjoyed hearing it." She grasped the elderly woman's gnarled hand. "I spoke with your daughter as I was coming in and she said you would be going home tomorrow."

The white-haired woman turned her head away from Annabella. "Not home. I'm not happy about that one bit. It will be the first time in sixty years...not since my Henry carried me over the threshold, that I haven't been in my own home. I raised ten children in that house."

"I understand how you must be feeling, Mrs. Cobb—"

The white head turned back, gray-blue eyes flashing. "I mean no disrespect, Miss Barton, but you do *not* understand a thing. None of you young blades of grass do. I am an old woman and I just want to be left alone to die in the same place I have lived most of my life."

"Mrs. Cobb, you broke your hip when you fell and you will need care. You will not be able to get around by yourself anymore." Annabella patted the fragile hand. "If you are with your daughter she can help you if needed."

"I know you think that is the best answer for this...but I know better. My Hetty is a terrible housekeeper. Do you know where they are stashing me?"

Annabella shook her red head in the negative.

The pursed lips tightened further. "In the room off the back porch, where they used to keep the potatoes. I will freeze before the winter is over." Mrs. Cobb sighed and gripped Annabella's hand. "Now, have I not been ungrateful? The good Lord has kept me on this earth for almost eighty years. He gave me a good husband to share life with and ten children to keep me busy. I am just a little sad and lonely with so many of them going on before me. It should not be that way, you know. A mother should not outlive her children."

Annabella smiled and leaned down to give the tissue-paper cheek a kiss. "I most certainly agree with you, Mrs. Cobb. I will be praying for you."

"Everyone always promises those words, but you can make my day a little brighter, Miss Barton."

Annabella laughed at the twinkle in the older woman's eyes. "And how may I do that?"

"Hetty's house is close to the trolley car line. It would not take but just a little bit of time for you to come and see me there and continue your reading in Paul's writings. I would surely love that."

"I think I can manage to work it out. You have Hetty ring my Aunt Agnes's house when you are all settled. I would love to continue our reading sessions."

A tear slipped from the elderly woman's eye. "You have made me a very happy old woman, my dear."

Annabella gave her a smile and wave as she turned to walk down the corridor of beds to the door leading from the ward. She pulled on her leather gloves and managed to walk right into the dark-haired, masculine form passing in the hallway.

A strong hand gripped her elbow, steadying her after their collision. "Please excuse me, miss. My thoughts were on other matters and I was not paying attention."

Annabella gave a light laugh. "I am sure I was at fault. I should have been minding my steps rather than my gloves." She met the dark eyes, so close to her and gasped.

"Annabella? Annabella Barton?" Orin Langworthy dropped her elbow and stepped back, his dark gaze sweeping over her.

"Why, why yes, you remember me?" Annabella clutched the front of her cape together and tried to still the frantic beating of her heart.

He gave a deep laugh. "Remember you? Of course I do. How could I forget that glorious hair and those amazing green eyes? We were supposed to be married, if I remember correctly. But that is hard to accomplish when you are standing before the preacher by yourself." His black mustache twitched with the last words.

Annabella searched the hall up and down before turning to Orin. "What are you doing in St. Louis, here at City Hospital?"

He chuckled once again. "I do come to St. Louis quite often on business, if you recall. I have an old friend that has been ill with pneumonia. I have tried to visit every day. He is doing much better. Thank you for asking." He smoothed his black mustache with his finger, his dark eyes glittering. "What brings you here? I pray it is not something terrible."

"No, I visit patients here, read to them or just sit with them so they are not by themselves. It can be a lonely place and a little scary if you are not feeling well."

"I would assume most hospitals would have that same problem."

Annabella stole a glance and met his dark eyes and gasped again. "I cannot believe we have run into one another like this."

"Literally," he smiled.

She looked away and clutched her cape once again. "After so many years."

"Ten years this May, to be exact."

"I know full well how many years it has been, Mr. Langworthy." Her green eyes flashed as she looked at him. "I just cannot understand why we would meet again after all this time."

"I cannot say that I am sorry." His eyes caressed her red hair. "I have purposely stayed away from Rubyville. I have not wanted to cause you anymore distress after that…unfortunate evening."

Annabella stepped closer to him and narrowed her eyes. "You stayed away from Rubyville because my father warned you to and you know it. You have never been a coward before, why now?"

He gripped her elbow firmly and steered her around the corner to a lesser traveled hallway.

She shook his hand away. "What are you doing? You cannot just waltz back into my life and take charge. Who do you think you are?"

He stepped closer to her. "I am the only man that *had* and *still has* the courage to marry you, Miss Barton."

"Maybe I am already married with several children by now." Annabella backed against the wall.

Orin pressed closer. "*Are* you married with several children?" When she looked away, he chuckled. "For all our progressive thinking and accomplishments, we live in a pretty small world. I know you reside on Lafayette Square with your Aunt Agnes and you both care for three orphaned children."

She gasped again. "Have you been asking around about me?"

"Not really. I have been here for a short time on business. People like to talk. You just have to listen."

"Then you already *know* I am not married and have no children. Why are you provoking me and why would it matter to you?" Annabella tugged at the wrist of her leather glove and smoothed the material.

"I am not the one that ran away." The words were spoken soft and low.

"I did not 'run away', Mr. Langworthy. I could not make a commitment to a man that had done what you did. I did not want to spend the rest of our marriage wondering where you were each time you were late for dinner."

"As I said, that was unfortunate and I am sorry that I hurt you. It was a very grave mistake on my part. I wish I could go back and make the correct decision, but I cannot." He touched her gloved hand. "I have had many years to regret my indiscretion."

Her flashing green eyes met his once more. "So you bump into me here and apologize and everything is just supposed to be alright? We can just begin where we left off?"

"Believe me, Annabella, if it were that simple, I would beg it of you. But I do not have those expectations. I am just as surprised as you that we met today. I never dreamed that I would see you again. Now that I have..." His voice trailed off softly. "Now that I have, all those feelings are still there."

Annabella ducked her head. "Please do not say those things now...not here. I do not know what the correct answer is or what I should be feeling. I just know I cannot trust you."

He touched her hand once more. "Then let me try to regain that trust. We enjoyed one another's company at one time. Maybe we can again. Just give me the opportunity to make it up to you."

Annabella smiled at the older nurse passing by. The nurse stopped and looked at Orin, her eyes narrowing. "Is everything all right, Miss Barton?"

"Oh, yes, yes, this is an old friend of mine from Rubyville. Mr. Langworthy is here in St. Louis on business." She turned to Orin and nodded. "So good to see you again, Mr. Langworthy. I pray your friend is doing much better today." She turned and walked swiftly away, rounding the corner to the large hallway that led to the front of the hospital.

AGNES SET HER CUP on the saucer. "If this isn't a barrel of pickles! Do you really think Mr. Langworthy is serious about wanting to see you again?"

Annabella nodded and crumbled more of the shortbread on her plate. "He said he wanted to try and regain my trust. He said all the feelings he had for me were still there."

"Do you believe him?"

Annabella closed her eyes and gripped her hands together. "I want to *so* badly. When I saw him today I could not even think or talk. All those old feelings for him were rushing at me and I could not even breathe. He was so handsome, standing there with his black hair, a touch of gray at the temples, those black eyes that seem to look right through you. Mr. Pratt has never made me feel like that."

"So you were attracted to him."

"Yes, but it was so much more than that. There is a fire, an excitement that I do not have with Mr. Pratt. I felt alive again and challenged."

Agnes took another piece of shortbread from the dainty china and placed it on her plate. She sipped her tea slowly, and sat back in her chair. "I think you should agree to see Mr. Langworthy again. Give him a chance to prove his love, if that is what he is still feeling for you. You cannot wonder the rest of your lives if you should have been together. You will both be miserable."

Annabella sighed and brushed the crumbs from her fingers. "That is what I have been thinking as well. That is what I *want* to do. I never would have thought he would still care for me after all these years. I do not want to miss this opportunity if we are supposed to be together." She stood from her chair and placed it against the heavy, mahogany table. "Now I need to know what to do about Mr. Pratt. I do not think he will take this latest turn of events very well."

"I think you are right. You will just have to explain the situation to him. He knows you were once engaged to the man and that you left him at the altar. If he cares about you at all, he will want this worked out in the best way possible…even if it means losing you."

Chapter Three

February 1896

I WAS WONDERING WHERE my valentine had disappeared to."
Annabella crossed her arms and gave a mock frown.

"He's just borrowing it for a bit, Mama Bella. Beth drew him a big
heart, but he can't make the naked baby." Ruth's big, brown eyes
drooped and she shook her head. "He's just not a good drawer."

Arthur scowled at his sister. "I am *too* a good drawer! Mama always told
me so." He looked up at Annabella, one brown curl bobbing on his forehead.
"But Ruthie's right. I can't draw that naked baby. Aunt Agnes gave me this to
put on the card." He held up a strip of lace. "But I can't make it stick."

Annabella smiled and tousled Arthur's brown curls. "Let me see if I
can help." She pulled a chair over to where the brother and sister sat at
the large, mahogany table. "You must have someone pretty special in
mind to give this Valentine to."

Ruth nodded, her eyes big and round. "Arthur is sweet on Lillian."

"Lillian Beckett, the pretty little girl in my Sunday school class?"
Annabella aimed the question in Arthur's direction. He ducked his head
and concentrated on his picture.

Ruth nodded again. "He said she's *be-you-tee-full*, with her yellow hair
and all." She clasped her hands at her cheek and fluttered her lashes.

"I did *not* say that!" Arthur looked up from his picture long enough
to scowl at his sister.

"Yes you *did!*" Ruth frowned back and stuck out her lower lip, her
brown eyes turning to black. "You did *too* say she was beautiful!"

Annabella bit her lower lip. "I think it is best that you do not argue.
It is perfectly all right to think a young lady is beautiful, Arthur."

He paused with his work and looked up at Annabella. "Aunt Agnes said I was too young to be sweet on anyone. She said I needed to keep my mind on more important matters, like school work."

"Well…you *are* young. It is also very important that you do well in school. But I do not think there is anything wrong with liking someone, or thinking they are a little more special. I think Aunt Agnes would agree with that as well." Annabella sat down at the table. "I think Lillian will be quite pleased to receive such an attractive picture from an admirer."

Arthur beamed.

"But he still can't draw that naked baby." Ruth tapped a stubby finger on the blond, curly-haired Cupid.

Annabella gave a light laugh. "First of all, it is not a 'naked baby'. It is called Cupid."

Arthur scratched his head. "I was wondering why a baby would have wings and then carry a bow and arrow. It didn't make much sense to me. But I thought it must be alright since Mr. Pratt gave it to you."

"The picture is just a way to let a person know that you think they are special. Sometimes Cupid is on the picture because he can shoot an arrow at someone and make them fall in love. Valentine's Day is about being in love."

"Does that really happen? Did Cupid shoot an arrow at you, so now you love Mr. Pratt?" Arthur screwed up his face and stuck out his tongue.

Ruth nudged her older brother in the arm. "You know Mama doesn't like you doing that. She said tongues were meant to stay in our mouths."

Arthur glared at his sister. "I already know that, *Ruthie*. You aren't the boss of me."

"Okay you two, no more squabbling. Let me answer Arthur's question before I forget what he asked." Annabella glanced at the two sets of brown eyes watching her. "Cupid does not really shoot an arrow at someone. It is just kind of a fun way to look at it, rather like a fairy-tale."

Arthur shook his head again. "Old people sure have strange ideas about things. Our papa told us to love people because God first loved us. Not because a baby with wings shot an arrow at us." He shook his head again.

Ruth wagged her head as well. "Not because of an arrow."

Annabella smiled and smoothed her hand over Ruth's long brown curls. "You two are much smarter than I am. We should get back to the task at hand. I think we have some mucilage we can use on that lace. We want it to stick well and not come off."

Agnes entered the dining room. "Mr. Pratt is waiting for you in the front parlor, Annabella. He will be staying for tea."

Annabella sighed and rose from her chair. She smoothed the fabric at her tightly corseted waist and patted the hair at the back of her neck.

"I won't be able to finish my valentine without your help." Arthur held up the piece of lace.

"I will help you, since Annabella has a visitor." Agnes took the seat beside Arthur and pointed to the red heart on the paper. "I think that lace would be lovely right here. What do you think?"

Annabella whispered a "thank you" to her aunt before walking slowly from the room, her wide skirts rustling against the floor. She took another deep breath and grabbed the ornate molding around the door leading into the front parlor. *Please God, give me the words to say to Mr. Pratt. This is not going to be easy.*

"Miss Barton, it is so good to see you again. You have not been at your usual places the past couple of weeks. I was beginning to fear that you had taken ill." Thomas greeted Annabella with a smile, extending his hand. He walked her to the green, velvet sofa. Annabella took a seat and arranged her skirts.

"I *have* been at City Hospital more frequently. The cold weather seems to make a difference in one's attitude. I want to spread cheer wherever I am able." She looked up and gestured for him to take a seat at the opposite end of the sofa.

He smoothed the collar of his gray-checked ditto suit and sat down, his long legs bent awkwardly. "I have heard that you take the trolley car each week to visit with Mrs. Cobb."

She nodded. "Yes, she is staying with her daughter, Hetty. We have been reading through all of the Apostle Paul's writings. It has become a very special time for me as well. She is a lovely woman. It is amazing to me that she has such fortitude at her age. She has been through so much." Annabella smoothed the tight curls at the base of her upswept hair. "Have—"

"Have you—" Thomas cleared his throat. "I am sorry, you may proceed."

"No, really, it was of no importance. I would like to hear how you have been. It *has* been awhile since we visited." She gave him a smile and folded her hands in her lap.

"Yes, several weeks as a matter of fact." He cleared his throat once more, his pale face reddening with the effort. "Have...have you been avoiding me, Miss Barton?" His gaze focused on his knee.

"No, I have not. I have just been more busy than usual with the hospital visitations. As I said earlier, the winter weather seems to bring more sickness with it and makes people dispirited."

"I have seen you with him, walking through the park, visiting the shops. You appear to be so happy to be with him, always laughing, your cheeks glowing. You have never been that way with me."

Annabella's shoulders sagged and she gripped her hands together tightly. "His name is Orin Langworthy. He is the man I was to marry almost ten years ago."

Thomas scratched at his knee with one long finger, following the movement with his pale-blue eyes. "I had surmised as much. It is what I had feared." He pushed back onto the sofa, his back board-like against the tufted cushions. "I care for you very deeply, Miss Barton. I had prayed and hoped that you would be my wife. We could continue with the work we have been doing together here in St. Louis. We could even adopt Arthur and Ruth...give them a good, solid home. I know Beth would like to stay with you as well. She could be part of our fam—"

Annabella raised her hand and placed it gently on Thomas's forearm. "Please, do not make this any more difficult than it already is. I care for you as well, but...it is just not the same way in which I care for Mr. Langworthy."

"Maybe we need more time to get to know one another?" His eyes, lined with pale lashes, reached out to her and gripped her heart.

"We have known one another almost *five years*, Thomas. We work together several days a week, we attend the same church. I am fairly certain we understand how the other thinks and feels on almost every subject."

"And that is why I am asking you again to think of marriage. I have not wanted to be forward or inappropriate, but I love you, Miss Barton.

I want you to be my wife. I will not consider another."

Annabella shut her eyes and squeezed back the tears. "Please do not say that. You deserve a wonderful, caring, loyal woman by your side. Someone that admires and loves you for all the talents you have."

"You are saying you feel none of those things for me?" His voice caught on the last word and he cleared his throat once more.

Annabella stood and crossed her arms at her narrow waist, gripping her sides. She paced before the fire, her movements pushing air against the flames. They sparked and flared with each passing. "I care for you, Thomas, but I do not love you. Not in the way a woman should love her husband. I admire and respect you, but I do not have the same feelings for you as I do Mr. Langworthy." She paused her pacing and held her hands before her bodice, her palms facing him. "Please do not make me hurt you anymore than I already have. I want to be your friend and continue as we have been doing for the past five years."

He shook his head and raised his long length from the velvet cushions. "I cannot do that any longer. I want you by my side in all ways. I am willing to wait a while longer. Maybe you will see the value and wisdom in all that I have said." He walked slowly to the foyer and took his overcoat from the brass hook upon the wall. He put it on, adjusting the velvet collar. His eyes met her own. "I will be praying for you, Miss Barton. Please remember that you left that man at the altar...and for good reason. I may not be as handsome or as wealthy. You may not find me as exciting to be with, but I am here and I have been for five years. You may trust me with your life...can you do that with him?" He placed his top hat upon his thinning hair and exited the house, the cold, winter air swirling into the room.

Annabella shivered and felt the sadness in her heart, a tight gripping of pain spearing through her chest.

Chapter Four

March 1896

Y OU ARE MOST CERTAINLY not in the best form today, my dear."
Orin tilted his dark head and slid his right arm along the back of the
park bench. His dark eyes caressed her face. "You have refused to let me call
on you and now when you agreed to walk with me, you will not speak. I think
your little friend Beth has conversed more with me." He nodded to where
Beth and another girl strolled with arms linked, talking and gesturing
excitedly. The March wind was cold, but neither girl seemed to mind.

Annabella smiled and watched the two young girls. "Beth was so
excited to see Melanie here. They spent a lot of time together at the
home...the best of friends. I know she has missed her."

Orin patted her chin with his gloved finger. "As I have missed you. After
seeing you at the hospital, I had hoped you would allow me to call on you. I
was very disappointed when your aunt said you were not accepting callers."

Annabella pushed her hands further into her sable-lined muff. "I
needed some time to think and make some decisions. I am afraid I have
hurt someone very dear to me and I do not know what to do about it."

Orin leaned back against the wood slats. He stroked the elaborately
carved, ivory handle of his walking cane. "Is this person of the male or
female gender?"

"He is a man I met about five years ago. We attend the same church.
We have worked together, helping at the children's homes, visiting
hospitals, and taking food to the poor. He has been a very good friend
to me. Always there to help whenever needed. The children love
him...he always has funny stories to share."

"If I understand correctly, this man has feelings for you beyond being a 'friend'." Orin leaned the wood cane against the park bench and smoothed his mustache, his right hand tapping against the slats.

Annabella nodded. "His name is Thomas Pratt. He…he cares for me and wants me to be his wife."

Orin tilted his head and looked at Annabella once again. "Do you love him? Have you accepted his offer of marriage?"

She shook her head. "I have not accepted his offer. He had given me a beautiful Valentine card, shortly after I had seen you at the hospital. I have known for awhile now that he had feelings for me, but that card made it very clear. After that conversation with you, I knew I could not marry him."

He leaned forward, his dark eyes searching her face. "Why?"

Annabella sighed and met his gaze. "I have always known that I did not love Mr. Pratt. But I ventured to think we could have a life together and raise a family. I think in time I would have loved him. He is a decent and caring man, very loyal, and a hard worker."

Orin chuckled. "You are not employing him to work in a shop. You are speaking of marriage."

"Marriage is not only about love; many other attributes are involved in a good marriage."

Orin threw back his head and laughed. "Spoken as someone that has never been married."

"*You* have not been married either, Mr. Langworthy. So you are no more an expert on the institution than I am." Annabella's cheeks flushed red and she shifted her position to turn from him. The wind tossed the black feathers perched on her hat. They danced and dipped against her upswept, red curls.

Orin stood and pulled the velvet collar of his overcoat higher against his neck. He took his walking cane and reached out his right hand. "Come, it is cold sitting on the bench. You can fluster and fume as we walk." He smiled as she took his hand and stood. "You come by that red hair honestly. I have never encountered anyone that can spark as quickly as you can, my dear."

She shied away from him and stuffed her hands back into the muff. "Well, for some reason, you are the only person that seems to have the ability to do that to me."

He chuckled as they walked along the brick path. "I am happy to hear you have feelings for me."

Annabella 'harrumphed' and scowled.

"So," he continued, "you do not love this Mr. Pratt, but you think he would make a good husband and in time you could love him. But after seeing me again, you cannot marry him." He stopped and turned to her. "Is that what you are saying?"

Annabella stopped as well and smoothed a long curl from her cheek. She looked up at him and nodded. "That is the conclusion I have come to."

His eyes darkened and swept over her face. He leaned close and lowered his voice. "So I will ask you again, Miss Barton...why?"

Annabella's cheeks flushed a deeper red, her green eyes turning to liquid. Tendrils of red escaped and danced before her face, catching on her moist lips.

He reached out and gently swept the hair away, his gloved finger hesitating at the corner of her mouth. "You are so beautiful. You have come to me in my dreams, laughing and dancing, your glorious hair swaying at your hips."

Annabella turned away, brushing at the escaping curls before covering her trembling lips. "You should not speak of such things."

"I should not tell you how I have missed you? Our rides beside the stream in Rubyville, talking with you, making plans for our future, building the house that was to be our home? No woman has ever fulfilled me and challenged me as you do. I love you, *still*, Annabella. How can I make you understand that?" He gripped her elbow and turned her to face him.

She brushed at the tears slipping over her cheeks. "How do you expect me to believe you? I miss all those things you mentioned as well. I could not stay in Rubyville because of all the memories of you. I had to leave and try to start my life over, even though every part of me wanted to remain with my parents, in the town they founded and built. You took that all away from me, Orin Langworthy! All because of an 'indiscretion' as you call it."

She turned and walked swiftly away, her head bent against the wind. She left the brick path and sought shelter against a large oak tree, the tears falling freely.

He strode to her side and positioned himself so she was blocked from the view of others walking along the path. "I cannot make that night go away. What I did was wrong—"

"I *heard* you with Maggie Peters! I had to stand there and listen to you *with* her, saying things to her you should have been saying to me!"

Orin stepped back. "You saw us and remained there?"

She brushed at her cheek and sniffed. "I could not see much because it was dark, but I certainly heard you. You telling her how beautiful she was...kis...kissing her. You should not have been doing that the night before we were to be married! How could you?" She stomped her foot and seethed, her chest rising and falling rapidly.

"Why did you not say something? Make your presence known?"

Annabella narrowed her eyes and hissed, "Do not blame this on me, Orin Langworthy. None of this was my fault." She brushed at her red nose. "What was I supposed to say? 'Here I am, out on a midnight walk, just seeing what my betrothed is doing? Please excuse me, but could you both stop touching one another?' Really, how perfectly ridiculous can you be?"

Orin reached into his pocket and pulled out a white handkerchief. He held it out to her. "If you were 'listening', then you know nothing went beyond a few kisses."

Annabella snatched the handkerchief and blew her nose with a loud 'trumpeting'. "I *know* no such thing. I covered my ears and waited until you both left the gazebo."

He chuckled and smoothed his mustache, while shaking his head. "All these years."

Annabella gripped the used handkerchief into a ball. "I do not think this is a laughing matter."

"Oh, believe me, my dear; I do not think it is either." He positioned one hand against the tree, tapping his cane against the frozen ground. "All these years, you thought I had consummated an act with Maggie Peters?"

She nodded. "What else was I supposed to believe? You should not have been there at that time of night with that...*girl*. Everyone in Rubyville knew what kind of person she was. She was always on the hunt for a wealthy husband."

"Everyone, and that includes me, my dear. Nothing happened between us. Just those few kisses you must have heard. If you had really listened, you would have known that I stopped what was going on and told her I was not interested. After a few choice words, she left and then I walked home... *alone*. No, I should not have been there with her. But I could not sleep, so I walked over to the park for a little fresh air. She was there. I should have left immediately, but I did not. She caught me in a moment of weakness."

Annabella stared at him, her eyes wide. "You expect me to believe all that? You are telling me that nothing really happened and I walked out on our wedding for no reason?"

He shrugged and changed his position against the tree. "If you heard us, I can understand why you were upset. I was not too pleased with myself. I had every intention of telling you what had happened whe—"

"*When* were you going to tell me? A few years down the line? Maybe after I caught you with someone else?" She stuffed her hands into the muff and raised her chin, looking away from him.

"I was going to tell you that night, after we were married and alone. My conscience would have not let me be with you until I had confessed what had happened. You have to believe that, Annabella. I loved you, still love you and I wanted to be with you and start our life together."

She swung back and faced him, her green eyes snapping fire. "I do not *have* to believe anything! You ruined our lives, Orin Langworthy! You ruined them on a few kisses."

Orin's dark eyes met hers. "As I said at the hospital...I'm not the one that ran away."

"Mama Bella, I was wondering where you were." Beth skidded to a stop, her eyes shifting between them. "I did not mean to interrupt. Melanie had to leave, but it was so wonderful to see her." She stretched her arms out and smiled. "And look, it's starting to snow."

They tilted their heads to the sky, small flakes drifting to their eyelashes. The wind had stopped and gray clouds hung low.

"It is indeed," noted Orin's low voice. His gaze turned to Annabella. "We should continue this conversation at a later date. I will walk you both home before the weather turns worse."

"But it is so pretty out right now. Can't we stay a little longer?" Beth looked between the two, her blue eyes pleading with a flutter of lashes.

Annabella smiled. "None of that, young lady. Aunt Agnes will be expecting us for tea." She gave a shiver. "I am about frozen anyway, a warm fire sounds delightful."

Orin offered his arm to Annabella. She glanced down and pursed her lips.

Orin raised a brow. "Now none of that, *young lady*, the bricks may be slippery. I would never forgive myself if you fell and had to wear a goose egg on your head." He smiled down at Beth's laughter and offered his other arm to her. She took it with a toss of her golden curls and snuck a peek at Annabella.

Annabella sighed and grasped Orin's arm. "This is not over by any means," she whispered.

He smiled, his black mustache lifting at the corners. "I know, and I cannot tell you how delighted I am." He gave her a wink and continued his conversation with Beth.

ANNABELLA SNUGGLED DOWN DEEPER in the warmth of her bed. The ornate, cast iron radiator in the corner of the room had cooled, leaving a chill in the air.

'You are so beautiful. You have come to me in my dreams, laughing and dancing, your glorious hair swaying at your hips.' Annabella felt her face flush, warming to the tip of her nose at the remembered words. She buried her face in the white pillowcase and groaned. *You should not be thinking of such things in the middle of the night! You should be praying. Heaven only knows how little of that you have done lately! God has been a far-away thought the past few months.*

She flipped to her back and pulled her arms from the covers, lacing her hands atop her tummy.

Dear, Heavenly Father, I know I have been too busy of late to talk with You. Yes, I know I make a good show of praying when I am with the children at the home or Mrs. Cobb, but I have not really talked with You in so long. Please forgive me. I can be a very selfish woman…but You already know that! I know I do not deserve to even have You listen to me, but I need Your help and guidance. You know what a mess I have made of my life. You know I left Orin on our wedding day and changed our entire future. I did that because I thought I was justified because of what he had done.

Annabella groaned and shifted to her left side, her hand beneath her cheek.

I think I was wrong, Father! Now what am I to do? Thomas wants me to be his wife. I trust him and I know he would be a wonderful husband and father. He loves You and lives his life according to Your Word.

Orin's tanned features flitted through her head, his black mustache lifting at the corner with his smile.

I cannot get Orin from my mind and heart. I keep remembering all those days in Rubyville, the long rides by the river, and our talks about all sorts of things.

Did your conversations center around Me and the plans I had for you?

I know Orin loves You, Father...he just does not show it as much as Thomas does. But he does care what You think.

Do his plans center around My Word and what I would have him do?

Annabella squeezed her eyes tight. *But I love him, Father. I know he loves me as well. He can take care of me, provide for me, probably better than Thomas can. He already built a house for me. We could go back to Rubyville and have our lives there as we always planned.*

Does his love for you come second to the love he has for Me?

Annabella sat up, drawing her knees to her chest. She gripped them tightly.

Yes, Father, I know that Thomas would answer all those questions correctly. But I do not feel the same for him. He does not excite me...make me want to jump for joy like Orin does. Should I not be bubbling over with happiness when I am with Thomas if I am meant to marry him? Should my heart be racing each time I see him or hear his voice? That is the way it feels to be in love...right? I thought that was what love was, the way it made you feel.

Do you love *Me*, My child?

The words came to her, softly, drifting through the chilly air of the room, and disintegrated.

Chapter Five

April 1896

MRS. COBB SAT ON the front porch of the little, two-storied house. She rocked back and forth, a brightly colored quilt upon her knees.

"I thought I might find you out here today." Annabella greeted the white-haired woman with a smile as she climbed the three steps to where she sat. "The trees have tiny green leaves on them and the birds are singing. It is a beautiful spring day in St. Louis."

Mrs. Cobb threw back her head and gave a hearty laugh for one so frail. "You always brighten my day with your smile. April is a glorious time of year, is it not? Everything is new and green after a long, cold winter." She narrowed her eyes and looked past the gingerbread trim of the porch. "If I was at home, I would be planting my garden by now. I always tried to get it in early. There was just something about getting my hands in that soil, feeling it cool and moist, sifting through my fingers." She patted the vacant rocking chair beside her own. "Come sit down, my dear. Hetty said she would bring some tea in a moment."

Annabella placed her worn Bible on the small table between them and took a seat in the offered chair. "How are you feeling?"

"The doc was over a couple days ago. He says I am mending just as I should." She pointed to a cane resting against the table. "He brought that for me, said I should be able to get around a little better with it. It does not feel any too good though." Mrs. Cobb shook her head. "I will just have to bear the pain; it will not be the first time. Birthing ten children showed me that."

"Here is your tea, Mama." Hetty swept onto the porch, a large tray held high. "Good afternoon, Miss Barton. I did not know you had arrived."

"Just a minute or so ago," Annabella updated, taking her Bible from the table. "I may have taken a bit longer to walk from the trolley today. This glorious weather puts you in the frame of mind to enjoy it."

Hetty set the tray on the table with a rattle of china. She mopped her brow with her large, white apron, her next words muffled by the muslin material. "Yes, it would be nice to just sit and visit for a bit." She dropped the material and set a red, thin hand upon her scrawny hip. "But I have laundry to finish up. The clothes are drying well with this spot of warm weather."

"You know you are always welcome to join us in our Bible reading. We would love to have you." Annabella smiled up at the plain features of the older woman.

"Well, thank you again for the invite, but as I told you before, I do my reading and praying on Sunday, just when the Good Lord wants me to. Now is the time to work. So, I will be getting back to my chores. Let me know if you need anything, Mama." Hetty tucked the quilt more firmly about her mother's knees. "Make sure you stay covered. There is just enough of a breeze that you could chill, and then you would be sick. I do not know how I would fit that into my busy day." She swept from the porch, her brown hair pinned into submission. Not a strand floated on the breeze.

Mrs. Cobb shook her head as she reached for the tea pot. "Ten children and the one with the demeanor of a scalded cat is where the Good Lord placed me." She paused in the pouring of the tea and looked off into the distance. "Hetty always was a sour puss. My Henry and I never understood why she ended up that way." She shook her head again and set the pot on the tray, offering a cup and saucer to her guest. "Life just never held much joy for her. Even going to church is like having a tooth pulled."

Annabella smiled and took a sip of tea. "She takes very good care of you."

Mrs. Cobb scowled and waved a hand at Annabella. "She does not have a thing else to do. I dare say I have made her life busier by being here, but the girl needed it; keeps her mind off her troubles." She leaned forward and whispered, "Her house is cleaner too. With me here she has to stay home and not gallivant from house to house visiting with all the neighbor women." She 'tsked-tsked' and shook her head. "In my day you stayed home and cared for your family, made sure your house was spotless. You did not have time for trading gossip."

Annabella set her cup on the saucer and placed it on the tray. "She makes good tea as well."

Mrs. Cobb chuckled, her brown eyes dancing. "I see what you are doing, my dear. Yes, Hetty does make a delicious pot of tea. And yes, she has taken very good care of me. I do need to be thankful for that. I could not have been at home in this condition. The Lord provides."

"Yes, He does…it is just hard to know what is *His* provision versus something we may want." Annabella played with the long row of tiny buttons at her wrist.

"Are you speaking of that young man that has come into your life once again?"

Annabella nodded, "Although I do not know if Mr. Langworthy may be called 'young'. He will be forty years old this year."

"Oh pshaw! He is still young enough to marry and have a family…just as you are."

"I celebrated my thirty-third birthday just a couple of days ago, Mrs. Cobb. That is not 'young' for a woman by any stretch of the imagination. Having a family at my age seems pretty far out of my reach."

"You do not have one foot in the grave either, my dear." She smiled at Annabella and held out one gnarled hand. When Annabella placed her hand in the older woman's, she gripped it tightly. "Now you listen to me. You have become a daughter to me. Maybe God sent you to help ease the ache of losing my last little girl when she was just a few hours old. But I am rambling again." She squeezed the hand she held and closed her eyes, leaning her head against the back of the rocking chair. "I had a slow start as well. I married when I was twenty years old. When I look back now, it seems like I was barely out of diapers, but as you know, I was heading toward spinsterhood."

Annabella laughed and rocked slowly back and forth, the gentle breeze lifting the tiny curls framing her face.

"My Henry and I managed to add to our family just about every two years. I had a little more of a break between the last couple, and no more after our littlest girl died. She was just not ready to be born. She was *so* tiny…fitting into Henry's two hands. I was forty-four then and thought my heart would never heal from the hurt of losing a child." She brushed at the tears slipping from her closed eyes, following the wrinkles of her face. "We did not know then that the war would be starting in another year and it would take five of our boys from us. One of them was much too young to even be thinking of going to fight, but he did." She shook her head and sat straighter in her chair.

Annabella smoothed the tears from her own cheek. "I am so sorry, Mrs. Cobb. I had no idea."

The older woman opened her eyes and smiled at Annabella. "Of course you did not, my dear…it is not something I share readily." She patted Annabella's hand and released it. "What I want to say is this. Our time here is filled with joy and heartache. The Good Lord knows what you can handle and He has a purpose in it. I can look back over all my eighty years and see that now. Just remember to listen to His words, read His book and keep in prayer. He will guide and direct you." She gestured to the worn Bible in Annabella's lap. "I think it is time for this old woman to stop talking so we can hear more from Paul's letters."

ANNABELLA NEARED THE THREE-STORIED house on Missouri Avenue. Laughter carried on the wind and she looked up to see her aunt trying to ride a safety bicycle. Her wobbling movements and near tumbles were causing the children great amusement.

Ruth ran to Annabella and grasped her hand, pulling her along the walkway. "Aunt Agnes is learning to ride a bicycle, and she isn't doing very well."

Annabella smiled. "I can see that. I pray we have no broken bones before she has accomplished the task."

Agnes placed both feet on the ground and slowed to a stop in front of Annabella. She straddled the bicycle, catching her breath. "Do you want to have a go at it?"

"You *have* to try it, Mama Bella. I did and it was so much fun! I did better than Aunt Agnes did." Beth looked to Agnes for confirmation.

Agnes brushed at her brown hair, smoothing it away from her flushed face. "That she did. It just takes an old horse like me a little longer to learn a new trick. But I will be riding this all over St. Louis before summer's end, I will guarantee you that."

Arthur crossed his arms before his chest and scowled. "I didn't get to try yet."

Annabella placed a hand atop his brown curls. "I think that bicycle is a little tall for you. You would not be able to get on."

"Well, I could sure try, couldn't I?"

Ruth shook her head. "You shouldn't, Arthur. You will fall off and crack your head open, just like Aunt Agnes is always saying. *I'm* not going to try."

"That's because you're just a *little* girl. You can't try." Arthur leaned down and jabbed the point home with a stare at his sister.

"I'm not much littler than you!" Ruth accentuated each word with a drop of her chin.

Agnes held up a hand and silenced the brother and sister with a stern look. She slipped her leg over the bar and fluffed her skirts. "I think I will need to purchase one of those bicycling costumes, maybe some bloomers. These skirts are a little long and cumbersome for such activity." She turned to Arthur and Ruth. "I think with Annabella's help we can give you both a short ride."

Arthur gave Ruth a conquering grin.

Agnes held up one finger at Arthur. "But ladies first." She gestured for Annabella to take the handlebar of the bicycle and she gripped Ruth under the arms, swinging her to the seat of the bicycle.

"I don't know if I want to try, Aunt Agnes." Ruth gripped the material of Agnes's leg-of-mutton sleeve. "I don't want to crack my head open."

Annabella placed her left arm around Ruth's small form, while holding the handlebar with the other hand. "We will not let you fall, Ruth. You just have to trust us and relax."

Agnes positioned herself the same way on the opposite side and they slowly started walking. "Is this not fun?" Agnes asked, her brown eyes twinkling as they glanced at the little body perched upon the seat.

Ruth grinned, the dimples on her rosy cheeks deepening. "More fun than I thought." She looked back at Arthur, standing beside the tall oak tree, tapping his foot upon the ground. "But I think it's time for Arthur's turn."

"Alright, we will turn around and you can ride back to Arthur." Agnes steered the bicycle in a wide circle and headed back.

They repeated the procedure with Arthur, his wide smile and glittering brown eyes declaring his excitement. "When I am bigger, I will have one of these bicycles and I will ride with you, Aunt Agnes."

Agnes laughed. "Is that so, Mr. Marlow?"

He nodded. "But my name is Arthur. Mr. Marlow was my papa's name. I thought you knew that." Arthur glanced between the two women, his arms draped across their shoulders as they guided the bicycle down the walkway.

"You were being such a gentleman that I felt I should address you as a gentleman. Since your last name is Marlow, you will be called Mr. Marlow when you are older, just like your papa was." Agnes took a deep breath. "I think I am just about worn out. I have been sitting beside the fire all winter enjoying the warmth like a cat and eating too many tea cakes. I am not in the best of shape."

The two women laughed and stopped beside the large oak tree, helping Arthur to dismount. Annabella leaned the bicycle against the tree and patted her face. "It *is* a little warm today for all this exertion."

"It is your turn," reminded Beth. "You have to give it a try."

Annabella widened her eyes and gave a loud sigh. "I would like to, but I am pretty tired. It is springtime; there will be plenty more days for me to try it out."

Agnes set her thin hands on her flaring hips and tapped her fingers. "I think you are afraid." She raised a brow and gave a half-smile. "If an old woman like me can learn to ride, you certainly can."

Annabella grabbed the handlebars and walked the bicycle to the road. "Well, of course I can!" She flung a look at her aunt, "And I am *not* afraid!" She lifted the skirt of her gray walking suit and slid delicately onto the seat. She put one black leather boot on the pedal and pushed off with the other foot.

"She's doing it!" Arthur shouted as Ruth clapped her hands.

"She *is* a bit jerky, but she really seems to be doing well. Much better than I did," Agnes said as she took Arthur and Ruth by the hand. "Shall we walk a bit on this nice, warm day? The weather might not be so fair tomorrow. April can be rather indecisive that way."

"What does, inde, indec—" Arthur frowned.

Beth shook her head. "Indecisive means that you cannot decide what to do. Aunt Agnes is saying the weather—"

"How do you stop?" Annabella slowly rode past, the bicycle wheel wobbling with Annabella's corrections.

"I just put one foot down at a time and drag it until I stop!" Agnes called as Annabella traveled away from the quartet.

Annabella turned her head back. "Please repeat what—" The front wheel hit a large root just as Agnes shouted for Annabella to steer clear of the tree. Annabella was tossed at the huge maple, coming to sit in a heap at its base. She pushed her hat back to the top of her red bun, brushing at the black feather that dangled from the side.

"Are you alright, dear?" Agnes rushed to her side and knelt beside Annabella, checking her face and arms for damage while discreetly pulling her skirt and petticoat over her leather-clad ankles.

Annabella nodded, the feather bobbing up and down at a crazy angle.

Agnes began laughing, covering her mouth to hide the merriment. "That *is* another way to stop, but I would not recommend it. I think the most damage you sustained is to your feather."

"It broke," Ruth stated solemnly, staring at the drooping decoration.

Annabella reached out a hand and gripped Agnes's hand as the older woman helped her to her feet. "My pride did not fare so well either." She smoothed down her skirts and winced when she turned to do the same on her backside. "My nether regions are not so good. You would think with all these layers I would have been offered a bit of padding." She presented her back to Agnes. "Would you please brush me off? I fear I have last autumn's leaves adorning me."

"You have a long tear in your skirt," informed Beth, helping to pluck leaves from the gray material.

Annabella sighed and shook her head. "I should have changed from my best walking suit before trying such shenanigans." She brushed at the feather once again. "My hat will never be the same."

"That is easily repaired," stated Agnes. "Beth may work on her sewing skills while you soak in some hot water. With the tiniest of stitches, you will never know the tear was there." Agnes frowned, "The mud is another matter. It may be difficult to remove."

"Well, I wouldn't have run into that ole tree if it were me." Arthur struggled to pick up the bicycle.

Beth grabbed the handlebars from Arthur. "Since you are too short to ride, I guess we will never know."

"I won't be short for long. Someday I will be bigger than you." He bent over and straightened his black knickers.

"And how do you know that?" Beth gripped the handlebars and tossed her blonde hair.

"Because boys are always bigger than girls when they're older. Mr. Pratt is bigger than Aunt Agnes and Mama Bella. Don't you know anything?" He shook his head and positioned his flat cap over the brown curls.

"Hush, you two, there is no need to squabble over every little thing." Agnes looped her arm through Annabella's. "Right now we need to get Annabella home. Arthur, take your sister's hand, and Beth, you bring the bicycle. You saw where I had it in the carriage house."

"Well, until I met with the tree, I was rather enjoying myself. With a little more practice I think a bicycle would be a very useful mode of transportation." Annabella climbed the stairs to the house, wincing with each step. "I fear I am going to be a bit stiff and sore for a couple of days."

"You're always saying that you aren't as young as you used to be," Arthur reminded. "I'm falling and running into things all the time and it doesn't bother me a bit."

Ruth nodded. "He falls all the time. He fell out of bed just last night."

Agnes helped Annabella into the house and ushered in Arthur and Ruth. "I thought I heard a 'thump' last night."

Arthur grinned. "That was just me. Didn't even crack my head open."

Agnes wrapped him in a big hug. "That is because you have such a hard head. But I love you anyway."

She pressed a kiss upon Ruth's forehead. "Now scoot, both of you, while I help Annabella. I think you both have a bit of homework to finish before school in the morning."

"No, ma'am, I finished mine before we went out. It's Beth and Ruthie that have homework." Arthur stood with his cap in his hand, slapping it against his knee.

"Then you may read until supper." Agnes smiled at his "Yippee!" She looked down with the tug at her skirts. "And what might you need?" she asked Ruth.

"I can't make the letters on my homework. Teacher said I have to practice and practice. But they don't work." Ruth pushed out her bottom lip.

Beth entered the long hallway that divided the house from front to back. "Mr. Jacobs said he would put the bicycle away when he was finished."

Agnes rubbed her forehead. "I had forgotten that he said he would be doing some cleaning. He likes everything tidy for the warm weather." She patted Ruth's shoulder. "Ruth needs some help with her letters. I am going to see to Annabella and then help Mrs. Jacobs in the kitchen. With all the excitement, supper will be a bit late."

THOMAS WATCHED AS THE two women and children entered the house.

I pray Annabella was not hurt. That was a pretty serious tumble off that contraption.

He walked from the growth of bushes that had been his covering while observing the antics of the little 'family' he had once spent much of his time with. He continued his walk through Lafayette Park, passing the heavy iron fence that surrounded the park as he turned left onto Lafayette Avenue.

I do not know what to do, Father. I want to give Annabella time to decide what she desires for her life. I know she does not love me, but I think she cares for me. We could have a very fulfilling life together. I refuse to believe she does not see that. She has to remember what that Mr. Langworthy did...how he betrayed her. She is a smart woman. I will have faith that she will make the correct decision. She is just flirting with freedom right now, wanting what she cannot have. But she will come to realize how wrong that Langworthy fellow is. She will come back to me. We will be married.

He swallowed deeply around the knot in his throat. *She is all I want in this life, Father. I cannot imagine living without her. Please bring her back to me. Please, Father. I know you have plans for us.*

Chapter Six

"HAVE YOU MADE YOUR decision?" Orin took a seat on the carved rosewood chair and crossed his legs.

"What decision was *I* to be making?" Annabella turned with a sweep of her skirts and sat on the sofa. She smoothed the mint-green day dress over her lap and folded her hands.

Orin smiled and tapped one long finger on the arm of the chair. "I do understand if you are disgruntled that I had to leave the city on business. I admit that it was very poor timing. I had hoped that after our discussion in the park a few weeks ago—"

"It was March…almost a month ago."

He nodded. "Yes, it was."

"I do not recall that I was to make a decision, only that we were going to continue with our *discussion* as you called it." She raised her chin and focused on the cold, empty fireplace.

"I had asked you why you could not marry Mr. Pratt, even though you had come to the conclusion that he would make an adequate husband for you."

"If *my* memory serves me correctly, you had just finished telling me that I had left you standing at the altar for no good reason." She threw her hands in the air. "Now, almost ten years later you are making me feel as though I was an empty-headed little, little—" She crossed her arms, her chest heaving as she stared at him. "I do not even know what to say."

"Then please answer the question that I have asked several times." His eyes darkened as he smoothed his mustache above his lip.

"You will not leave me be until you hear the words, will you?" Her green eyes turned to liquid. "I still love you! That is why I cannot marry Mr. Pratt."

She brushed at the tears slipping down her pale cheeks. "And now you tell me what an idiot I have been all these years, making decisions based on something that was not true." She pointed a long finger at him and shook it. "Even though you should not have been doing what you were doing."

Orin stood and walked to the sofa. He sat beside her and took one hand in his own, turning her to face him. "As I said that day in the park, I was so very wrong, Annabella. I know I hurt you deeply. But we can begin again, or even continue where we left off. I still love you and want to be with you. I do have business elsewhere that I have to see to now and then, but we could reside in Rubyville for much of the time…if your father allows me back in town." He said the last with a half-smile and a twitch of his mustache.

Annabella looked down at their clasped hands. "I just feel so foolish. I was so angry with you. I ruined our lives with my decision to act out of my hurt."

He lifted her hand, and placed a kiss upon the pale, freckled skin. "Our lives have taken different directions than they would have all those years ago. But they have not been ruined. I have been very successful with the railroad and you have a very fulfilling life here with your aunt. I have seen you with Beth, Arthur, and Ruth. You love those children as your own. So nothing has been ruined."

Annabella sniffed and brushed at the tears. "I…I just cannot forget about that night. The words you said to her, and the sound of you kissing one another. It made me feel just…*awful.* I do not want to experience that again…*ever.*" She looked up at him, her green eyes brimming. "I love you, Orin, but I will not stand for anymore of your *indiscretions.* Do I make myself *very* clear?"

He reached out and touched her wet cheek, dabbing at the moisture. "*Extremely* clear, my dear. I have felt terrible for ten years, wondering why you had left me, missing you and wanting to find you again." He reached into his pocket and handed her a handkerchief.

She brushed at her nose and folded the white material into a tidy square. "You have always known where I was. You know my parents live in Rubyville, rarely leaving and you know my aunt lives here. I do not think much effort was put into finding me."

He shrugged. "Maybe not as much as I would have. Your father warned me to leave you alone and to stay away from Rubyville. I would not have been welcome to come calling. I assumed your aunt felt the same way." He leaned back against the tufted cushions and draped his right arm along the intricate carvings of the emerald-green velvet sofa. "You also have to remember that I did not know why you had run off the day of our wedding."

"I cannot believe my father let you leave Rubyville without knowing. He was very upset with your behavior as well."

"He may have been. He did not inform me of the reasons why you left me standing at the altar, only that you had been very hurt and he did not want me around to cause you anymore pain."

Annabella met his gaze. "So what are we to do now?"

"I want you to be my wife, just as you should have been all those years ago. I love you, Annabella. I love your spirit, your determination, and I love the way we fit together. We were made for one another." His eyes darkened and his right hand caressed her shoulder. "I think we could have many, many happy years together."

Agnes entered the front parlor with a clearing of her throat. "I do apologize for interrupting, but Mr. Pratt is here, Annabella. He said he has something urgent he needs to speak with you about." Agnes looked pointedly at the hand resting against Annabella's mint-clad shoulder.

Orin dropped his hand as Annabella stood. "I can speak with him in the foyer."

Orin stood as well, adjusting the checkered vest he wore. "If it is not too much to ask, I would like to be introduced to the man that has been such an important part of Miss Barton's life for so many years." Orin glanced at Annabella. "You have told me so much about him."

Annabella smoothed the stray hairs at the base of her neck and pulled at the frills of her high collar. "Of…of course, I am sure Mr. Pratt would be delighted to be introduced to you as well. Please invite Mr. Pratt in, Aunt Agnes."

Thomas entered the front parlor, his top hat held at his side. He nodded to the intimate group.

"Mr. Pratt, may I present you to Mr. Langworthy? He has been known to our family for many years." Agnes spoke as she gestured with an open palm to Orin.

Orin held out his hand. "I have heard much about you, Mr. Pratt. It seems you have been a delight to Miss Barton and Miss Saunders, and the children as well. Beth has mentioned you many times."

Thomas shook the hand offered. "Yes, I have heard of you as well. I pray you are enjoying your time in our fair city."

Orin smiled and sought Annabella's eyes. "As a matter of fact, I have just returned from a month away. I had some business to attend to. But, yes, I am enjoying St. Louis immensely. Thank you for asking."

Annabella pulled her gaze from Orin, clasping her hands before her waist. She turned to Thomas. "Aunt Agnes said you had something you wished to speak with me about."

Thomas cleared his throat, his face reddening. "Yes, one of the girls at the home was taken to City Hospital just a short time ago. Because of the nature of her illness, I felt I should request your presence with me to visit. But since you are otherwise occupied," he turned to Agnes, "I would ask that Miss Saunders would accompany me if possible."

"Well of course, Mr. Pratt. The children will not be home from school for a couple hours yet. Just let me inform Mrs. Jacobs of my plans. I will return in a moment." Agnes glanced between the threesome before exiting the room.

"May I ask who was taken to City Hospital?" Annabella addressed Thomas. "Was it serious?"

Thomas cleared his throat again and looked down at his feet. "It is Mary."

Annabella gasped and placed one hand to her chest. "*Mary*...sweet Mary, she did not lose—"

"I am ready, Mr. Pratt." Agnes entered the room, adjusting the ribbons of the light cape about her shoulders.

Thomas focused his gaze on Annabella. "Yes, she did. There was much loss of blood and...and she is not doing well." He turned to Agnes. "We should hurry." He gestured toward the foyer and followed the older woman from the room.

Annabella backed to the sofa and dropped to the cushions below. She leaned her elbows on her knees, placing her hands over her face. "Not sweet Mary. She has been through so much."

Orin walked to her side and laid a hand against her back. "Would you like me to take you to the hospital?"

"I should have gone with them. I was just so flustered by what we had been talking about that I could not think clearly." She looked up at Orin. "And then you were here and I did not want to upset Mr. Pratt anymore than he already was." She shook her head. "I seem to be messing everything up whatever way I turn. I do not know what to do next."

"Is Mary someone that you are close to?"

Annabella nodded. "She is one of the older girls at the children's home. Or I should say she was. She went to live with an older woman back in February." She covered her face with her hands and rubbed her forehead. "She is only fourteen years old. She has had a very difficult life. Her mother left her when she was only a baby and she has lived with her father and her uncle…her father's younger brother. Her uncle was inappropriate toward her." She sat back and crossed her arms. "She was expecting a baby in just a few weeks." Annabella's shoulders shook with the emotion as she started to cry. "She is so young…much too young to raise a child. But she was so excited about the baby. She said she wanted to be a good mother, not like the one she had had."

Orin knelt before her, his left hand on the arm of the sofa. "Let me take you to the hospital. Then you can see her and comfort her."

She shook her head. "No, I had best remain here. The children will be home soon. Aunt Agnes and Mr. Pratt are close to her as well. I can see her tomorrow." She wiped the tears from her eyes with the handkerchief she had been given earlier. "I seem to be doing a lot of crying today. I must look a fright."

"You are beautiful as always, my dear." Orin's gaze swept her face and the untidy curls escaping her upswept hair.

Annabella gave a half-smile. "Well, I thank you for the compliment, but I think you are going blind in your older years. I have never been beautiful and when I cry, my face turns red and blotchy."

"You have always been and will always be beautiful to me, Annabella Barton." Orin smoothed a curl from her cheek and brushed a finger across her bottom lip. He cleared his throat and stood, shoving a hand in his pocket. "I think it is best if I leave. We can continue our conversation of today after you have found out how young Mary is doing." He went to the foyer and took his trilby hat and walking cane from the brass hook upon the wall.

Annabella stood and walked slowly to the foyer, watching as Orin placed the hat upon his dark head. "When will I see you next?"

He gave her a smile. "Soon, my dear, very soon." He opened the front door and turned to her once more. "Remember that I love you, Annabella…only you."

ANNABELLA PACED THE SMALL room where she, Agnes, and the children enjoyed breakfast each day. The three children had left for school amidst the chatter and bustle that characterized each school morning. She gripped the front of her wrapper as she listened to her aunt relay the events of the previous evening.

"So you never had a chance to talk with Mary before…before she died?" Annabella's voice caught on the last word.

Agnes took a sip of her tea and set it gently on the saucer. "No, by the time Mr. Pratt and I arrived at the hospital, they had her in surgery, trying to stop the bleeding. They were not successful." Agnes sighed. "The baby was stillborn…a little girl, just like Mary had prayed for."

Annabella stopped her pacing and gripped the back of a chair. "Why would God allow the life Mary had? Why would He allow the suffering of any of the children we see on a daily basis at the home or on the streets?" She made a fist and pounded it against the dark wood. "I just do not understand, Aunt Agnes. Mary lived such a horrible life with that monster she called a father and then the unspeakable things her uncle did to her." Her voice broke with the emotion she was sharing. "Mary treated everyone with such love and consideration. When she was at the home she cared for the younger children as if they were her own family—"

"They *were* her family, Annabella…the only family she ever really knew." Agnes interjected gently, sniffing back her own tears.

"And then when she went to live with Miss Ulster because her pregnancy was showing, she was nothing but grateful for a nice home to live in and food to eat. She never demonstrated bitterness or anger toward the people that made her life so miserable for her short fourteen years on this earth." Annabella shook her head. "I just cannot understand it."

"I do not understand either, my dear. But God knows the purpose behind what He allows in our lives. He knows the plans He has for us and He says they are for our *good*. So I trust that and have faith in what He tells us in His Word." Agnes took the cloth napkin from her lap and laid it on the table.

"Are you not angry about what has happened with Mary?" Annabella stared at her aunt.

Agnes closed her eyes and sighed deeply. "Yes, I am very distressed about losing Mary. I wish she had had a very different life. But because of that life with her father, she was sent to the home and we had the opportunity to share God's plan of salvation with her. I know she accepted Christ as her Savior and that she is in Heaven now…as is her baby girl." Tears slipped from the brown eyes. "I know they are happy together and the trials and strife of this life are over for them. That consoles me and gives me hope for all the children we care and pray for." She returned Annabella's gaze. "I thank God for the few months we had with Mary. She was a very special, young woman."

"I should have been there, Aunt Agnes! When Mr. Pratt told us what was going on, I should have left right then and there and accompanied you to the hospital. I have been so caught up in my own life and struggles…that seem so small now." Annabella dropped her head and rubbed her temples.

"There would have been nothing that you could have done except sit and wait for many hours just as Mr. Pratt and I did. The children needed you here to help with their homework and have supper with them. I know Ruth was delighted that you read her bedtime story to her. It is a change from the usual."

Annabella walked to the window and pulled aside the lace curtain. She leaned her head against the ornate molding surrounding the glass. "It is such a beautiful spring day, the bright green of the trees leafing out, and all the flowers in bloom. I am sure the lilacs and peonies planted around Mama and Papa's house in Rubyville are just starting to burst with fragrance." She sighed and reached up to slide her hand down the thick, braided length of hair hanging to her waist. "The sun keeps on shining and the birds singing, even though we hurt on the inside."

Agnes pushed her chair back and stood as she smoothed the shirtwaist she wore. She walked to the long window and stood beside Annabella. "I am so very happy for that. I do not want everything to stop when I have a trying time or bad day. Life must go on, my dear. You know that as well as anyone." She wrapped an arm about Annabella's waist and hugged her, placing her cheek against the chintz material of Annabella's arm.

"I know I seem ungrateful, but I have been so appreciative of these years here with you, helping at church and the home. The children that have become a part of our lives for even a short period of time have blessed me in so many ways." She looked down at her aunt. "I would not have had these opportunities if I had stayed in Rubyville. I would probably be a bitter, old woman by now, miserable in my spinsterhood. My mother would be distressed every day because I was not married and settled down."

Agnes laughed. "That she would."

Chapter Seven

I *ADORE* SATURDAY MORNINGS!" Beth skipped alongside Annabella, her golden hair bouncing against her back.

Annabella smiled as she watched Beth's antics. "And why is that? Why is a Saturday morning any different than say a...Thursday morning?"

"You know why," Beth tossed back with a giggle. "There is no school on a Saturday and no church, either. Aunt Agnes gives us permission to sleep in just a bit later on a Saturday...*and*," she stopped skipping and slowed to a walk, "I get to spend the day with you." The pink-cheeked face looked up. "My most favorite person to be with... *of course!*"

Annabella laughed and offered a greeting to those they passed on the crowded sidewalk. "I think most of St. Louis is out enjoying the beautiful day we are having. I have not seen so many out and about in a long time." She glanced down at the blonde head. "Well, I am flattered that you enjoy being with me. I enjoy your company as well." She reached out and took the hand of the twelve-year old in her own gloved hand. "You have been a part of our lives for a long time now. I do not know what Aunt Agnes and I would do without you."

"I do not ever want to find out." Beth slowed and gripped Annabella's hand tighter, a frown upon her brow. "I heard Aunt Agnes talking with one of the ladies at church. Does someone want to take Arthur and Ruth to live with them?"

Annabella nodded. "Even though you should not be listening to other people's conversations, you heard correctly."

"I do not think Aunt Agnes was trying to keep it a secret."

"Well, just remember to be respectful. It was not a secret, but it sounds as though you were not part of their conversation. Those that eavesdrop usually do not hear good things about themselves." Annabella looked down at the blonde head. "Aunt Agnes and I were going to speak with you, Arthur and Ruth this afternoon when we have tea. We wanted to inform you all at the same time. I fear the news will be difficult for Arthur and Ruth. Does it bother you that they will be leaving soon?"

Beth shrugged. "You and Aunt Agnes said they would be with us for only a short time, but they were different somehow. I mean, their mama and papa used to go to church with us and help at the children's home before they died in that fire." She shrugged again. "I just pray that God has a good family for them to go to. I want them to be happy."

Annabella leaned over and squeezed the girl to her side. "Arthur and Ruth will have a wonderful family. They will not be the oldest or the youngest but right in the middle of four other children. The father is a pastor and they live on a farm outside St. Louis. It will be a short enough distance for us to visit on a regular basis. I think they will be very loved and happy."

Beth beamed up at Annabella. "That is the best news! I have been praying. I have felt like an older sister to them. It made me really sad to think I would never see them again."

"God always works out the little details, even better than we could ever imagine."

Beth pointed to a dark-haired man and woman leaving a millinery shop in the block just ahead. "Is that Mr. Langworthy there?"

Annabella narrowed her eyes, scanning the sea of flowers, birds, and feathers atop the people before them. "Yes, I do believe that *is* Mr. Langworthy."

"Who is that woman with him?" Beth scowled and looked up at Annabella. "She has her arm linked with his."

"Yes, I do see that as well." Annabella pulled Beth close to the shop windows, away from the crowds. The awning extending over the sidewalk offered shadows to hide in. They watched as the dark-haired beauty placed a kiss upon Orin's cheek before climbing into the carriage at the curb of the sidewalk. The carriage angled onto the equally crowded roadway, the horses prancing in the sunlight. Orin glanced their way and then turned with a shrug of his broad shoulders before disappearing into the brightly-colored throng.

"Did you see what that woman did? She *kissed* Mr. Langworthy!" Beth drew her eyebrows to a point. "And in public as well!"

Annabella bit her lower lip, chewing upon it until the metallic taste of blood brought her to her senses. "We do not need to jump to any conclusions, Beth. She kissed him on the cheek."

"Does Mr. Langworthy have a sister? That is the only way a kiss would be appropriate."

Annabella shook her head. "Not that I am aware of. He does have one brother, but he was married to a much more petite, shall we say, not as pretty, woman." Annabella frowned. "If I recall correctly, she had brown hair, not black."

"Well then, who can that woman be?" Beth placed her hands upon her hips and looked up at Annabella. "I thought Mr. Langworthy loved you and wanted to marry you again."

Annabella sighed and rubbed her temple. "I think we should return home. I am not feeling well…a bit of a headache coming on. It must be all the crowds and warm weather." She looked at Beth's flashing blue eyes. "Would that be alright? I think Aunt Agnes will understand. We can purchase the thread she wanted another day."

"Of course, Mama Bella…I am sure Aunt Agnes will understand. She would have been upset as well if she had witnessed what we just did. If *my* intended had done that I would have something to say to him."

Annabella gave a half-smile and straightened her shoulders. "I am sure you would, my dear." *Not again, Orin…please do not do this again. My heart cannot take the pain of your betrayal. I know you love me, but why am I not enough for you?* She listened to Beth's chatter, feeling the tight grip around her heart as it squeezed until she thought she would burst.

"MISS BARTON," THOMAS POKED his blond head out the door and looked up and down the dark street. "Do you have someone with you, Miss Beth perhaps, or your aunt?"

Annabella shook her head and shivered. "May I come in? It has grown cold. I should have worn a heavier wrap."

Thomas ran his long, pale fingers through his thin hair, causing it to stand up. "Mrs. Scott has gone home for the day. It would not be…appropriate for you to come in with me here alone. I am sure you understand, Miss Barton." He stood in the doorway, his tall form blocking her entrance.

Annabella closed her eyes and pursed her lips. "Yes, I do understand, Thomas." She opened her eyes and squared her chin. "If I was worried about what was *appropriate* right now, I would not be here. I left Aunt Agnes's house, by myself, after dark, and walked over here *alone*. I need to speak with you now, before I change my mind."

"Are you sure it cannot wait until the morning? I could call on you after church…or I could walk you back home. Surely that would be enough time to talk with me. Your aunt must be very worried about where you have gone." His fingers brushed through his hair once again.

Annabella straightened and stepped over the threshold, pushing against Thomas as she made her way into the dimly lit foyer. "This cannot wait until morning. Aunt Agnes thinks I am in my room with a bad headache. I asked to not be disturbed until morning." Annabella gripped the heavy shawl she had thrown about her shoulders and shivered once again.

Thomas scanned the empty, dark streets once more and then slowly shut the heavy, walnut door. "We…we may speak here or in the parlor. I was just turning down the lights before I went upstairs. I will turn them up again."

"No, please leave them. The darkness is better right now. My head does not hurt as much."

She followed Thomas into the dimly lit front parlor and he gestured for her to take a seat on a tall-backed chair. She walked to the sofa and sat down, her back stiff and straight. "Do you still love me, Thomas?" The words came out stilted and cold.

Thomas backed to the wide, arched doorway leading into the foyer and stood, his hands hanging at his sides. "Of course I do. My feelings for you have not changed since we last spoke."

"Do you still wish to marry me?" Annabella stared straight ahead, her eyes unblinking.

"Well...well, yes I do...but you said you did not care for me in that way." Thomas spoke soft and low. "Have your feelings changed for me?"

Annabella shook her head and covered her face with her hands, her sobs shaking her body.

Thomas walked to where she sat and bent down, patting her back, his movements awkward and inept. "There, there, it will be all right, Miss Barton. Whatever the trouble is, God will take care of it. He is there for you."

Annabella looked up, meeting his blue eyes with her green gaze. The lashes were dark and wet against her pale skin. "I know He is, Thomas, but He seems so very far away. Do you ever have a bad day? Are you ever angry with someone? Is there ever a time when you cannot go to God with your problems?"

Thomas pulled up to his full height and stepped back. "Yes, I have days that are not as good as I would wish them to be. I have been angered by people in the past. But I do not want those times to control my life. God always works situations out for the best. His plan is best."

Annabella gave a short laugh. "I am not so sure about that, Thomas."

"You do not mean that. You are a strong Believer, Annabella. You have always prayed and relied on God to work out your problems. You have been a testimony to me over the years...your strength and commitment to what is right."

"It has not gained me anything of importance." The words were whispered low.

Thomas sat down and took her hand in his. "I do not know why you are here and so distressed, but I cannot allow you to talk so disparagingly. It cannot be that bad, Annabella, *whatever* is troubling you."

Annabella gripped his hand and stared into his eyes. "Do you still love me and want to marry me, Thomas?"

"Yes, I said that but a few minutes ago."

"Then I accept your proposal of marriage. We can be married as soon as possible." Annabella's eyes searched his face, darting here and there.

Thomas leaned back. "What has brought this on, Annabella...why the change of heart now, so suddenly?"

Annabella pulled her hand away and brushed at the tears upon her cheeks. "I saw him with another woman…this morning…when Beth and I were out running errands for Aunt Agnes. The woman gave him a kiss on the cheek, right there for everyone to see." The sobs came once again, her body trembling. "I thought he loved me, Thomas. I have loved him all these years. I was so happy to see him again. He wanted me to marry him." She looked up at Thomas, her eyes brimming and spilling over. "Did you know that…he wanted me to marry him…after all this time?"

"I am so sorry, Annabella. I hate to hear that he has done that once again…hurt you that way." Thomas swallowed deeply and cleared his throat. "But you cannot run to me because of what you saw. That will not make everything right or better."

"Why not?" she sobbed. "Why can I not have the same happiness as everyone else? I want someone to love me and be true to me. I want to have a family. I did not think I cared too much about all of that…but I do, Thomas." She shook her head. "It will be just as Mama said; I will be old and senile with no family."

"I cannot believe that. You are a smart and beautiful woman, Annabella. You will be married and have a large family one day…I am sure of it." Thomas patted her shoulder.

Annabella shrugged his hand off. "So you do not want me, either." She stated the words with no emotion.

"I did not say that. But I cannot take advantage of you…force you into something at your weakest point. I care for you too much."

She grasped his hand once more. "I have told you in the past that I care for you, Thomas. I was even thinking of accepting your proposal of marriage, knowing I would grow to love you. You have so many wonderful attributes. You are probably too good for me…but I would make you happy, Thomas…I would be a good wife to you and a good mother to our children."

Thomas pulled away and stood, running his fingers through his hair and pacing the distance of the room. "I know what you say is true, Annabella. But you are in love with Mr. Langworthy and you are only here because he hurt you again this morning. You are not here because it is a good decision for you."

Annabella rushed to his side, her shawl dropping to the floor. "I am here because I know it is the *best* decision for me." She gripped his upper arms and pressed close to his long length. "I have always respected you, Thomas…your honor and integrity. I have enjoyed being with you over the years. We have had many good times…have we not?" She gazed up at him.

"Yes, we have." He closed his eyes and groaned. "I want to spend all my days with you…the rest of my life with you. I want to raise a family with you, Annabella, but not because I am second choice."

He gripped her arms as well and opened his eyes, searching her face in the dim light. "I love you so very much, my dear. My heart aches for you."

He reached up and smoothed her cheek, his fingers lingering at the edge of her lips. "You are so beautiful. I admire your exuberance for life, your sparkling green eyes and red hair. Being near you is like a fire drawing me closer." He groaned again and pulled back. "I cannot be with you in this way, Annabella. It is wrong. I will walk you home. We can discuss this again…when you are calmer and there are other people around for accountability."

"I want you to kiss me, Thomas." She sank against him once more, laying her cheek against his chest. "I can hear your heart racing. I know you want to accept my offer for our life together. I know you want to kiss me." Her arms slid around his waist and she braced her hands against his lean back. "You feel so warm. I feel safe and secure when I am with you, Thomas. Please help me feel loved and wanted."

"Annabella," he groaned her name. "If you only knew what you are doing to me. You should not be here…not like this."

He bent down and lifted her against his long, lean form, pressing his lips against her cheek, her brow, and finding her welcoming lips.

ORIN LANGWORTHY STRODE ACROSS the bedroom of the Planter's Hotel, unbuttoning the vest he wore. He shrugged it from his broad shoulders and tossed it on the chair in the corner of the well-appointed room. He sat on the edge of the bed and took the tintype of Annabella off the small, mahogany table beside the bed. It was the likeness of Annabella that he had carried with him since their first engagement back in 1886. He studied the younger version of Annabella.

Your fire for life glows through. I cannot wait until we are husband and wife, experiencing all that life has to offer us.

He thought back over the day and the morning spent with his sister-in-law. His brother's first wife had passed away in childbirth several years before. It had taken him a few years to remarry and Orin was very pleased with his new wife, Laura. In many ways she reminded him of Annabella. It had been a pleasant morning shopping for hats. He was looking forward to introducing Annabella to Laura. He knew they would become as real sisters in no time at all.

Soon, Annabella…soon we will be together…finally, after all these years.

Chapter Eight

ANNABELLA STEPPED SLOWLY DOWN the stairs, her right hand holding tightly to the black walnut banister. She paused on the last step, her left hand going to her chest, stilling the frantic beating of her heart. The pounding beneath her striped shirtwaist continued and she took a deep, fortifying breath. *Give me strength, Father. Please give me the words to say to this poor man. I have used him in the worst way possible. I can only pray he will forgive me someday. Wretched woman that I am!*

She left the stairs and walked through the foyer, reaching the arched, wide door into the front parlor. Thomas stood at the window, one thumb looped on his vest pocket. The morning sun glinted off his mustache and short, pointed beard, silver threads among the gold.

He turned at the sound of her heeled boot upon the wood floor. He turned from the window and gave her a bright smile. "Good morning, my dear. I am happy to see that you are feeling better."

"Ye…yes, I think I was just overtired from all the excitement of the past week." She wrapped her arms around her corseted waist and gripped her elbows.

"I came calling last Sunday when you were not at church. I was concerned that after…well, after what happened the previous evening—" Thomas blushed red and looked at the floor. "I was worried that maybe you were not well or that I had hurt you in some way." He cleared his throat.

"I was fine, Thomas. You did not hurt me in any way. I was not up to seeing a lot of people…just needed a bit of time to myself to think and decide what to do." She walked slowly to the green, velvet sofa and sat down. "I do apologize for going to your house that night, Thomas. I should not have been there. I was hurt, lonely, and sad. I thought that being with you would help all that go away. I should not have used you in that manner."

He rushed to her and knelt on the floor at her feet. "You did not use me, Annabella. I was more than willing." He reached into his vest pocket and took out a small, gilded box. He opened it, to show her a ring, cushioned on a bed of white satin. "I want you to wear this until we can be married. It is just a small token of my love for you and to let everyone know that you are promised to me. I am afraid it is a little old-fashioned. It was my mother's ring when she was a young girl. I did not have time to have something made for you as I would have liked."

Tears slipped from Annabella's eyes and fell to the dark material of her skirt, leaving black splotches. "It is beautiful, Thomas…and…and very special that it was your mother's ring." She covered her trembling lips. "But, I…I cannot marry you, Thomas…not now."

He stared at her, his mouth open. "But we have to be married…immediately. You gave yourself to me and I have to make an honest woman of you, Annabella. I will not allow you to remain single after what we have shared." He took the ring from its satin bed and held it to her. "I love you, Annabella, and I want you to be my wife, as soon as possible."

Annabella scooted to the side and slipped from Thomas. She went to the marble of the cold fireplace and gripped the mantle. "I need a little bit of time, Thomas…time to think about what I have done and what I need to do now. I should not have used you the way I did."

"Stop, Annabella!" Thomas threw the ring and box on the sofa and stood. "You did not use me. I wanted you and have for a very long time. I do not regret the time we shared that night. But we have to be married quickly and make it right. You are *mine*, now."

Annabella turned and clenched her hands into fists. "I belong to no one. Not you…and not Orin." Her green eyes flashed and her chest heaved. "I am not some pawn to be moved around wherever someone else sees fit."

Thomas held out his hand. "You know I did not mean those words in the manner in which you took them. We have shared something that God meant for marriage. You have always believed that."

She shook her head and sighed, "I still do. I just need a little time." She rubbed her temples. "I feel so much shame for what I have done, Thomas. I used something that was to be shared between a husband and wife to make you feel as though you *had* to marry me. That somehow if I was with you in that way, Orin would no longer be an option as a husband for me."

"I understand what you are saying, but you also know that I love you, Annabella. What we shared was still beautiful and more than I had ever hoped for. Just do not sully it now with your refusal to marry me. I cannot bear it!"

"Oh Thomas, I am not refusing you, just asking for some time to get my thoughts in order." She walked to the long, front window and stared at the lace covered glass. "These past few months have been so very confusing for me. In my rational thinking, I knew I should marry you for all the reasons I have mentioned so many times before. But something was always holding me back. When Orin entered my life once again, I knew what that was. I had been longing for him, loving him still after so many years." She wrapped her arms about her waist. "I was so excited to think we were going to be together after all." She leaned her head back and closed her eyes. "But then I saw him with that woman and all those feelings of ten years ago rushed back…the betrayal, the hurt, and the anger."

Thomas walked to her side. "It was only natural you would feel those things. Anyone would have. Trust is earned and when it has been forsaken it is hard to regain."

Annabella opened her eyes and turned her gaze on Thomas. "I do care for you, Thomas. I care enough *not* to accept your proposal and ring right now. I want to accept them because I know I am doing it for the correct reasons. Not because Orin betrayed me once again or I committed an act with you."

She reached out her hand and laid it upon his upper arm. "I am going to Rubyville at the end of the week to stay for a month or so before Aunt Agnes comes with Beth. That will give me enough time to think and pray about what is best, without you or Orin clouding my mind. Now that Arthur and Ruth are settled into their new home, Aunt Agnes can handle things here until Beth is out of school. I did not want to leave her with so much responsibility before now."

Thomas rubbed the back of his head. "Will you return to St. Louis?"

"I honestly do not know right now. I know I can think better in Rubyville. My mind is clearer somehow. My father is there and he is a wise man. He will help me to get my bearings straight again."

Thomas reached out and took her hand in his. "Please remember that I love you. I want you for my wife and the mother of my children. I am willing to live wherever you think is best. We can continue our work here in St. Louis or we can live in Rubyville. All that matters is that I am with you." His pale, blue eyes searched her face, as if to memorize each feature.

THOMAS SET THE CABIN trunk on the ground and extended his hand to Agnes as she descended the trolley car. Beth jumped from the last step and looked up at the clock tower of Union Station. "We have just enough time to walk around a bit before your train leaves, Mama Bella."

Annabella stepped off the trolley with Thomas's assistance. "I am happy to hear that. With the crowds, I thought we might be running late." She gave Thomas a smile and "thank you."

Agnes scanned the crowds, her brown eyes jumping with excitement. "To think we have a place such as this right here in St. Louis. I have heard that hundreds of passenger cars go through here each day. Can you even imagine?"

"St. Louis must be about the best place to live in the whole world." Beth skipped alongside Annabella.

"It is most certainly one of the biggest cities." Agnes took Beth's hand in hers. "Young ladies should be more reserved. You can save the skipping for the park." She glanced at Annabella, Thomas walking beside her, carrying the cabin trunk. "I would have never thought to see such advancements in my day."

Annabella laughed. "Yes, it must be very changed from when you and Mama first arrived here back in the sixties."

Beth gaped up at Agnes. "You have been alive that long? Why, the Civil War occurred in the sixties."

Agnes smiled down at the blonde girl. "You are correct, my dear. My sister, Lavinia and I arrived here for the first time with our father on a business trip, just a few months before the War commenced. Our mother was not at all pleased with our Papa taking us on such a perilous journey in uncertain times. I was just ten years old…Lavinia almost fifteen."

"It surprises me to this very day that Mama would agree to go." Annabella gestured to an empty bench in a waiting area. "Why not sit for a bit before walking to the Midway? I know Mr. Pratt would appreciate setting down his burden."

"I am going to deliver your trunk to a baggage handler and I will return." Thomas nodded to Agnes, Annabella, and Beth before disappearing in the crowd.

They sat down, Beth situated between the two women on the wood slats of the bench. "It will be a long time before I see you again, Mama Bella." Beth stared at the multitude of passing people, her lower lip stuck out in a pout.

Annabella took her hand and patted it. "The time will pass very quickly. You have school to think of, and packing to do for the summer in Rubyville. Before you know it, you and Aunt Agnes will be here boarding the train for Kansas."

"But why do you need to go *now*? We always travel together."

Agnes met Annabella's gaze. "Annabella needs a bit of time with her parents before we arrive. So no more talk of the reasons why. You will see…the time will go quickly."

Thomas walked toward the trio, his long strides making short work of the distance. "Your trunk should arrive in Rubyville when you do, Miss Barton, provided the baggage smasher doesn't destroy it first." Thomas gave Annabella a smile.

"Thank you for seeing to that, Mr. Pratt. It always amazes me that my belongings arrive when I do." She gave him a smile in return.

Agnes glanced between the exchanged looks. "Well, our modern conveniences are truly amazing. No longer do we need to travel by covered wagon to arrive in Kansas."

Annabella looked up at one of the large, round clocks lining the wall. She stood, smoothing the skirt of her traveling suit. "Well, the time has come for me to go."

Beth stood and buried her cheek against the buttons of the short jacket Annabella wore. "I cannot bear for you to leave. Please let me come with you now. They will not miss me at school."

Annabella pulled away and placed one gloved finger beneath Beth's chin, tilting it up. "You will be missed and it is your responsibility to be there until the end. We will reunite again in but a few weeks. Then we will have a wonderful summer in Rubyville as we do every year. You will see it is just as I say." Annabella's eyes slid to Thomas's face, noting the set of his jaw and flushed cheeks.

"You will miss your train, Miss Barton." Thomas stated the words flatly, and cleared his throat.

Agnes took Beth's hand and placed her arm around her slender shoulders. "Now no more fussing...we need to walk with Annabella to the Midway and say our good-byes."

Thomas extended his arm to Annabella. She looked up at him, placing her hand at his elbow. "This will not be forever. I will write soon and let you know of my plans."

He placed his hand upon her hers and met her eyes. "I will be praying for you, Annabella. That God's will be done in your life. I pray it will include me, but I will also be praying for patience and acceptance for whatever you decide. Just remember that I love you, my dearest. Beth's wait will be nothing compared to mine."

Chapter Nine

May 1896

THE MID-MAY BREEZE SIFTED through the new leaves of the oaks and maples lining the park. The birds sang out to one another, joyous after the cold winter. Robins hopped through the grass, stopping to peck at the ground, occasionally pulling a long worm from the moist earth. The large, white gazebo languished in the center of the square, quiet in the early morning hours.

Annabella sat in the gazebo, a light shawl draped across her shoulders to protect against the slight, cool breeze. She had left her red hair to hang free, down her back, caught up with two combs at the side of her head, something she would never have been able to do in St. Louis. She breathed deeply and closed her eyes, letting the atmosphere and smells of Rubyville calm her soul, just as she had done every morning since her arrival four weeks before. She opened her eyes and looked east, across the park to see the sun begin its long ascent. The pink-orange glow could be seen between the leaves and branches, stretching into the dark sky.

My favorite moment in time, Father…when the day begins anew and all is hopeful and possible. The trials and tribulations from the day before are pushed aside in the glory of a new beginning.

As the sky lightened, Annabella reached for her Bible and began to read in the Psalms. The words quieted and calmed her soul, helping her to seek the answers she had been praying for over the past few weeks.

I often wonder what my love for Orin was based on, Father. Yes, I know he loved me, I know he would have taken care of me physically. Her eyes sought the copse of trees, just beyond the south side of the park where she knew the house stood that Orin had built for her and him to spend their lives in. *I even believe he loved You, Father. But I know Your thoughts were not his thoughts. Your way was not his way. He did not seek You first in all that he did and as a result, I did not either. Over many years together, that would have weighed on me, Father. So what was my attraction and love for Orin based on?*

She looked out over the park, her eyes drinking in the green and fresh beauty of the town her father had founded. She thought of the many people that had come to Rubyville, making it their home, and raising their families. She turned and looked north to just across the street where the limestone church stood. The very same church she was to marry Orin in. It was the church her family attended, built on land her father had donated. Each Sunday, they gathered with families in Rubyville and learned from God's Word and worshipped Him with music and prayer.

So much of Rubyville is me, Father. My very soul is built on the foundation of this town and Your Word. Did Orin ever feel that way? She closed her eyes and concentrated on the many conversations she had had with Orin over the years. He had been wonderful to talk with and they had so very much in common. He had always treated her with respect, admiring her knowledge and skills in areas that most women did not care about. *Is that what you loved about Orin...that he made you feel important and needed? He did not treat you as just another woman with silly ideals?* She opened her eyes and looked down at the words in front of her. *Surely that is important, Father.*

Important, dear child, but not everything in life or a marriage. You should not be so concerned with your own wishes and other's admiration of your skills, beauty and opinions. Living for Me, your actions a godly testimony, and your thoughts on things above are the important aspects of this life on earth.

The words came to her on the breeze, and she knew them to be true. *My thoughts and actions of late have been what is best for me and my desires. I haven't prayed, I haven't asked for Your leading on a regular basis...only when I feel panicked and in trouble.* She sighed and closed her Bible, placing it on the bench beside her. *And I treated Thomas the same way, Father.*

Her gaze settled on the limestone church. The steeple stretched into the trees, the gray slate roof glowing in the sunrise. The stained glass window above the double, arched doors leading into the building, reflected the rising sun, giving the colors a life all their own.

Annabella stood, arranging the shawl across her shoulders. She held it together, across her bodice as she bent and swept her Bible from the bench. She took the steps to the dew-wet ground and held her skirts from the dampness as she walked to the edge of the park and crossed the street in front of the church. She dropped her skirts and walked slowly up the sidewalk to the double doors. She set one pale, slim hand against the walnut and pushed the heavy door open.

She walked into the cool, dim foyer, and laid her Bible on the long table there. She pushed the door closed and preceded into the sanctuary, sniffing deeply of the wood interior, and the beeswax used on the pews. *It still smells fresh and new in here, although it was built over twenty years ago.* She thought back to the day when the first service had been held. She was only a child then, but she still remembered the importance of it being the very first church in Rubyville. It had stood tall and stately on the corner, the steeple seeming to touch the blue sky. Her father had given a dedication speech just before the pastor had preached the first sermon. The pews had been full, families and elderly bonded together and united in their one purpose to see God's Word taught in the growing town. She smiled as she glanced at the upright piano and remembered the joyful singing that had filled the sanctuary, seeming to burst at the confines of the room. *Such precious memories, Father. Thomas would appreciate them and be willing for them to become part of his life. Would Orin?*

Annabella turned at the sound of the church door opening and closing. "Good morning, Papa. I had forgotten that this was your place early in the morning."

William Barton laughed. "Never my place, Bella...the Lord's place." He bent and kissed her forehead, taking her hand in his. "You are more than welcome to join me in my devotions. Company every now and then is very welcome."

"I had been going through the Psalms in my own quiet time, just now over in the gazebo...but something seemed to be calling me here."

She glanced around the room, her eyes pausing on the tall windows and then pews. "I know this is only a building and that the Holy Spirit resides within us as a Christian, but there is just something very special about a church."

William walked her to the front pew and waited as she sat down before he took a seat beside her. "I could not agree with you more. I think it is because a church building is set aside for a purpose. It is for the gathering and teaching of the Saints, those that have accepted Christ as their Savior. I think the like-mindedness of all those Believers makes for a very special place to be. The presence of God is felt."

Tears slipped from Annabella's eyes, sliding down her cheeks. "I know God is with me always, but I fear I push Him away at times. The times when I think I can do alright on my own." She shook her head. "I have made so many very bad decisions, Papa. I know God forgives me, I know Jesus Christ died for my sins and paid the price…which makes my shame even worse."

William took his daughter's pale hand in his, the long fingers curling about her palm. "I know there has been something bothering you since you arrived home. I have waited, wanting you to come to me in your own time. The burden of guilt and shame is very heavy. Sometimes it is easier to deal with and heal once it is shared."

Annabella cried, her green eyes overflowing to spill down her lightly freckled cheeks. "You and Mama will want me to leave Rubyville when you hear what I have done. It will bring so much shame on our family."

William gripped her hand. "You are still here, so God must have a purpose."

Annabella looked up at her father. "I told you and Mama that Orin Langworthy was in St. Louis."

"Yes, and that you had spent some time with him." William reached into his pocket and pulled out a handkerchief. He brushed the tears from Annabella's cheeks and then gave it to her. "You also said that Mr. Pratt had asked you to marry him."

Annabella nodded. "Once I had spent time with Orin again, many of my feelings for him returned and I really felt he was the one I should marry. I told Mr. Pratt of my love for Orin as well."

"But Mr. Pratt led you to believe that he would wait for you if you should change your mind."

Annabella nodded again and blew her nose.

"Your mother and I felt that you had returned home to make a decision as to who was the best man for the job." His lips twitched. "Of course your mother is thrilled that you have two offers of marriage."

Annabella started crying again, taking in big gulps of air. "What I did not say was that I caught Orin with another woman…again. So I…so I went to Thomas's house and gave myself to him." Annabella gulped again, her shoulders shaking as she hung her head.

William released Annabella's hand and stood, his long fingers going to the back of his neck, moving in a circle. "So you *did* accept Mr. Pratt's offer of marriage?"

Annabella shook her head. "Not that night. When…when he called at the house a week later—"

"It took him a week to call on you?" William stood in front of her, his hands at his lean hips.

"No, he tried to call the very next morning, right after church, but I refused to see him." She sobbed again. "I needed time to think."

William paced the length of the pew, rubbing the back of his head. "If I understand, you were upset with Orin, *again*, after what you saw, went to Mr. Pratt's house and had…had relations with him and then refused to see Mr. Pratt the next day when he called on you." He stopped in front of her. "Annabella, look at me."

Annabella shivered and looked at her father. "Yes, Papa?"

"You gave your body to Mr. Pratt without the benefit of marriage?"

Annabella nodded. "Yes, Papa…just one time."

William shook his head and continued his pacing. "It is immaterial whether it was once or ten times. Because you were hurt," he stopped and shook a long finger at her, "by someone that had already done the same thing before, I remind you…you made a very bad decision."

Annabella gulped again. "I know, Papa."

William brushed at his red hair and rubbed his temple. "I am going to assume that Mr. Pratt called so that he could ask you to marry him?"

"He did…and I told him I did not want to marry him for the wrong reasons." She looked at her father's red face. "I did not refuse him, but I told him I needed some time."

William's face glowed redder. "Time…you needed more *time*? Maybe you should have taken some time *before* you went to see Mr. Pratt. Maybe you should stop and pray and just slow down any time you have an *emotion* coming on." William paced, his footsteps echoing on the wooden floor. "I do not know what to do with you, girl. You have always been quick-tempered and in a hurry. You do not think things through as you should."

"I know those are my weaknesses, Papa. I have always struggled with them." Annabella blew her nose once again.

"This time you have involved another person, Annabella. From what you have told your mother and me over the years, Mr. Pratt is a man of integrity and honor. I have a few choice words I would like to say to him concerning my daughter," he rubbed his red cheek, "but that will be for another time." He took a seat beside her once again. "I do not understand why you would refuse Mr. Pratt when he asked you to marry him."

"I did not refuse, Papa, I told him—"

"Yes, I heard…that you needed some time." He turned and took her hands in his. "You have already expressed feelings for Mr. Pratt and have told your mother and me that you believe he would be a good husband to you and father to your children. Orin Langworthy betrayed you, not once, but twice. Now you say you have given your body to Mr. Pratt as well." William looked into her green eyes and raised his voice. "What is there to think about? It seems to me you made your decision the night you went to Mr. Pratt's house."

Annabella nodded, glancing away from her father's own green eyes bearing into her. "I…I think you are right, Papa."

"You *think* I am right?" He gripped her hands. "Look at me, Annabella."

Annabella did as she was told. "You are correct. I had decided to write Mr. Pratt and accept his offer of marriage. It is the right thing to do under the circumstances."

Her father's green eyes, so like her own, darkened with her words.

"No, Annabella, it is the right thing to *do*. The circumstances have been of *your* making. You have involved many people in your bad decisions. When Orin betrayed you the first time, I agreed with you not marrying him and spending your life with a man such as that. Your timing...leaving him at the altar... was not the best way to handle it. But I supported you. I supported you all these years when you were in St. Louis. I felt you were doing good work there, a help to your Aunt Agnes. I was concerned about the relationship with Mr. Pratt you wrote of. I felt you were leading him down a merry trail. Now I know you were and that does not make me happy. I was most concerned when you wrote that Orin Langworthy was in St. Louis, but I felt you had been hurt enough to make the right decision where he was concerned."

William brushed at the curls stuck against Annabella's cheek. "Mr. Pratt has cared for you for a long time, Annabella. He wants to marry you. Since you have feelings for him as well, there can be no other decision made." He sighed. "Does your Aunt Agnes know of what...transpired between you and Mr. Pratt?"

"No...I led her to believe I was sick with a headache that night. I had gone to my room early." She swiped at her eyes. "She knows everything else, just as you and Mama did. She also thought I was traveling home early to make a decision where Orin and Thomas were concerned."

William sighed. "That is probably best. We do not need your mother upset with Agnes as well, thinking she had kept secrets from her." He patted her knee. "As I said, there is no other decision to make...you need to marry Mr. Pratt...if he will still have you."

Annabella nodded. "I knew you would help me to see things clearly and make the correct decision."

William slid his arm around Annabella's shoulders and pulled her against his chest. "My headstrong, independent daughter...you will most certainly be the death of me. Your mother was right, you know." He glanced down at her. "I have treated you more as a son than a daughter over the years."

Annabella looked up at her father. "I have not minded, Papa. I never wanted to be a simpering, thoughtless female."

"Just because you are female, you do not have to be simpering and thoughtless. You can be feminine and strong within the role God gave you on this earth. A man needs a strong woman to be his wife and support him through this life. Most men cannot survive without a woman by their side."

"I guess I have never thought of it in that way before." Annabella sat up and wiped the remaining tears from her face. "I do not think you will be having your devotions this morning. Mama will be wondering where we are *again*, and Martha will be waiting breakfast."

William stood and adjusted his vest. "Neither of which is a good way to start a day." He tapped her nose. "You need to write Mr. Pratt immediately and accept his proposal. Maybe we can have a June wedding in this church after all."

"My wedding to Orin was to be in late May, Papa." Annabella reminded him as they walked down the aisle of the church, their arms linked.

"Close enough. It only took ten years, but at least it's going to happen." William opened the door and they stepped out into the brilliant sunshine of the May morning.

Chapter Ten

WILLIAM RUSHED INTO THE front parlor, Martha close on his heels.

"Mr. Barton, you have left an awful mess on my floor." Martha wiped her hands on her white apron and placed the work-worn palms at her hips.

Lavinia set her embroidery on her lap and looked up at the flushed face of her husband. "Whatever is the matter, William? Your hair is a mess and you are going around in your vest." She gestured to the striped, gray vest he wore.

"I do not have time for all that nonsense, women! There has been a terrible calamity!" He gasped for a breath.

"What is it, Papa?" Annabella slid from the mahogany chair before the secretary and walked to where he stood.

He ran his long fingers through the tumbled mass of red hair. "I was just down at the train depot. They said a tornado hit St. Louis. They are calling it the 'Great Cyclone'."

Lavinia stood, her embroidery falling to the floor. "When did this happen?"

William shook his head. "I think they said it was Wednesday, around five in the evening."

Lavinia's plump hand went to her chest. "But this is Friday, William. Why have we not heard something before now?"

"The electricity and telephone lines are down. There were several fires." He looked at each woman in turn. "They said it is mass destruction, the worst tornado to ever hit."

Annabella grabbed her father's arm. "Oh, Papa…what about Aunt Agnes and Beth, Mr. Pratt and…and all those children at the home?"

William rubbed the back of his neck. "I do not have any other news. We will have to wait for more to come in."

Martha walked over to the sobbing Lavinia and placed an arm around her shoulders. "It will be alright, my dear. Little Agnes will be just fine...just you wait and see. She is a survivor, that one!"

Annabella covered her mouth with one shaking hand. "Do they have any names of those injured or dead?"

William shook his head. "Not yet...only that there were many dead."

Annabella pointed to the secretary where paper and pen lay. "I was writing to Aunt Agnes and Beth... letting them know that I was to marry Mr. Pratt. I received a letter just yesterday from him telling me how delighted he was that I had made my decision in favor of him. He was so very happy and looking forward to traveling with Aunt Agnes and Beth when they come in June."

William took his daughter's hand and patted it. "We will be praying that all is well. I can assure you they will have the trains running again as soon as possible. The three of them will be here before you know it."

Lavinia raised her head from Martha's shoulder and met her husband's eyes. "Do you really think so, William? I cannot bear to lose my only sister." Her eyes widened. "Do you think Jackson knows?"

William rubbed his forehead. "I would assume they have heard about this in Albany by now." He lowered his head. "Only God knows the outcome at this point. All we can do is pray for all the people. The lack of electricity and telephone service is bad enough, but people have lost their homes, businesses, and family members. It will take a very long time to recover from this."

"Come, my dear," encouraged Martha as she took Lavinia by the hand. "I will make us a nice pot of tea. That always lifts my spirits. The past few days have been so dark and gloomy, but it is cozy in the kitchen." Martha turned as they walked from the parlor. "You both are welcome, too. I made fresh bread this morning. With a spot of jam on it...well, it will work wonders."

"I will be in, Martha...thank you." Annabella gave the older woman a smile.

"I am going to go back to the train depot...see if I can hear of any more news. I will check the post office as well. The newspapers will have more information soon, I am sure." William kissed Annabella's forehead. "Spend a lot of time in prayer, Bella. These will be hard days ahead."

"THURSDAY, JUNE 11, 1896. My Dearest Family: I do apologize for the tardiness of this letter. It has only been two weeks since the 'Great Cyclone of 1896', but it seems as though it has been a lifetime. I pray this letter travels quickly to you, helping relieve the anxious thoughts I know you must be having.

"I will let you know that Beth and I are doing very well. We were at the City Hospital the evening that the tornado struck. The most ominous clouds had hung over the city that entire day and we decided to help at the Hospital rather than sit at home. The Hospital had been so overcrowded. Much of the Hospital was destroyed, but by God's grace, we were in one of the least damaged areas. It took us many hours to make our way home. Lafayette Park is no more. The huge trees are twisted, tangled masses of wood, the heavy iron fence around the park mangled as though it was a piece of tin. Lavinia, our parents' home survived better than most, but it suffered extensive damage. Almost the entire third floor is gone. What the tornado did not ruin, the deluge of rain finished, after the tornado swept through the city. Beth and I have been staying with dear friends from the church. We have been keeping very busy helping with the clean-up in the areas we are able, along with serving meals at the church."

Lavinia stopped reading and took the delicate handkerchief from her lap. She handed the pages of the letter to William. "I can read no more. Please continue." She dabbed at her nose and clasped her hands in her lap.

William glanced at Annabella seated beside her mother on the velvet sofa, and Martha, standing in the arched doorway of the parlor.

Annabella patted her mother's clasped hands. "Aunt Agnes and Beth are all right. I have been praying diligently that they would be."

Martha sniffed and cleared her throat. "And I as well...but those poor, dear people...what they must be going through!"

William walked to the turreted area of the parlor, and stood before the long windows draped in rose-colored velvet, angling the pages of the letter to catch the morning sun streaming in. He cleared his throat and continued the reading of the letter, his voice low and husky.

"It is with my very deepest regrets that I convey this next passage. Beth and I had searched and asked after Mr. Pratt anywhere we were able. We were given the news just yesterday that he had been visiting Mrs. Cobb at her daughter's house when the tornado struck. Mrs. Cobb's daughter, Hetty lived in one of the worst areas for devastation. Mrs. Cobb and Mr. Pratt both perished in the destruction. Hetty was able to locate us and let us know of the news. Apparently, she had been visiting a friend when the tornado struck and returned home many hours later to find it gone, only a pile of rubble left."

Annabella stared at her father, her eyes wide and unseeing. "Mr. Pratt and…and Mrs. Cobb? Both gone?" Her face reddened as she bit her lower lip.

William cleared his throat once again, taking a handkerchief from his pocket and brushing at his nose.

"I am making plans to leave the city at the end of the month. I would think the trains would be running efficiently again and I will have heard back as to the best course of action concerning the house. Many houses around Lafayette Park will not be able to be saved. Beth and I would like to remain in Rubyville past the summer, until I know what the Lord would have me to do.

"I write this with a very heavy heart and I know the news of Mr. Pratt and Mrs. Cobb will greatly sadden Annabella. Please know that we are safe and we are praying for all those here suffering, and we are helping as much as we are able. We pray for you as well. I will write when I have a more exact date of our arrival in Rubyville.

"Until then, may God be with you, and our love I send, Agnes."

ANNABELLA SAT GINGERLY UPON her bed, willing the nausea to go away. She lay back upon the pillows and placed one pale, shaking hand upon her tummy and closed her eyes. The early morning breeze lifted the lace curtains at the long windows. They floated up and down with each puff. The coolness drifted over Annabella, calming her clammy skin and damp hair.

Only one thing could make me feel this badly for so many mornings. She knew if she lay perfectly still, by the time the sun cleared the cottonwoods by the river she would feel good enough to move about slowly and dress. A nibble here and there from the bread served at the previous evening meal and hidden in a pocket would suffice until she made her way down for breakfast and the ever-questioning eyes of her mother and Martha.

They know something is wrong. I used to eat like a horse and now I can barely manage a cup of hot tea. Her red eyes began to tear up again. *I have cried for two weeks, Father. Every since we learned of Mr. Pratt's death and almost as many days of knowing his baby is growing within me. I cannot do it, Father! I cannot live this life I have made for myself! This burden is too hard to bear! I should have been the one perishing in that tornado. Not Mr. Pratt...a man of honor and integrity...only wanted to live for You. I brought him low, Father. My selfishness caused him to do something he knew was wrong.*

And now, the tears slipped quickly from her closed eyes and dampened the hair at her temples, *and now he will never know he was to be a father.*

She grabbed the pillow beside her head and covered her face with it, muffling her racking sobs.

If I was brave enough, I could press this until I breathed no more. Then all my troubles would be gone.

Would they, my daughter? Yes, you would be with Me, but what of your family? What of your baby? No...now is not the time...I have plans for you and your leaving of your life will be in My hands, and My timing.

Annabella pulled the pillow from her face and gripped it to her middle, cushioning the baby there.

I am a coward, Father! I cannot even walk the road that I have chosen for myself. Aunt Agnes and Beth will be arriving tomorrow and I will have two more people to try and explain things to. Now that was a cruel thought! To think that...after what they have endured the past month!

She turned her head to watch as the sky turned pink, topping the leaves of the cottonwood trees. *Another day, Father. Help me to use this one wisely and glorify You. I have so very many that I have not done that with.*

MARTHA POURED THE TEA into the cup, the gray swirls of steam emanating a delicious aroma.

Annabella took the cup off the saucer and held it to her nose, breathing deeply of the refreshing scent. "This is a bit different, Martha. It smells like mint."

"Yes, it is growing very well again, taking over my kitchen garden. It always helped your mother when she was expecting you." Martha hummed as she set the pot of tea on the table and proceeded to brush the crumbs from where William had breakfasted the hour before.

Annabella choked on the sip of tea, wincing as the hot liquid made its way down. She set her cup in the saucer with a crash of china and looked at the older woman.

"Do not be giving me that stare, child. I diapered your bottom when you were a baby and paddled it a few times, too. I know when things are not what they should be in your life."

She set her hands at her ample hips. "I also have taken care of your mama since she was young and helped her through more than one pregnancy. Those were hard times, losing so many babies...God bless their little souls. The spearmint always helped to settle your mama's tummy in the morning. It will pass and you will be fit as a fiddle in no time."

Annabella looked down at her lap and twisted the white napkin there. "How long have you known?"

Martha pulled out William's chair and sat down. "Maybe a little longer than you, but not by much."

She reached down and took one of Annabella's hands in her own, rough hand and squeezed gently. "I take it the child's father is the Mr. Pratt that lost his life in that tornado?"

Annabella nodded. "When I went to him that night, I did not even think of the possibility of this happening." She rubbed her forehead. "How could I be so stupid?"

Martha gave a chuckle. "Believe me, my dear it was not the first time and it will not be the last."

Annabella sighed and rolled her eyes. "Please do not say that. I am afraid that is very true, especially for me."

Martha patted Annabella's hand and then sat back in her chair. "You are no different than any of us. You just move more quickly, without thinking first. You have always been that way and it will lessen as you grow older and experience more of life. God has a way of purifying us. Each of us needs work in different areas."

"Well, I think the work He is doing on me is in vain." She looked at Martha, searching her blue eyes. "I am thirty-three years old. I should not be making stupid mistakes any longer. I knew that when I went to Mr. Pratt it was wrong, but I proceeded anyway." The tears slipped from her eyes. "Now he is gone and I will not have a husband and my baby will not have a father."

Martha sat up and shook her finger at Annabella. "That baby will have a father just as your papa and mama have more children than you, my dear. They just do not reside here." She pointed to the table and then clasped her hands on the white tablecloth. "The road will be more difficult of course, but that baby has you and a houseful of family here to care for and love him or her." She brushed at a crumb. "Your mama knows."

Annabella's mouth gaped open and she stared at Martha. "Mama knows I am expecting a baby?"

Martha nodded, wisps of her curly white hair bobbing.

Annabella continued to stare at Martha. "Mama knows and she has not said anything about it?"

"She talked with me a day or so ago about her suspicions."

Annabella lifted her cup and sipped her tea. "That explains why she has avoided me. I thought she was just preoccupied with Aunt Agnes's arrival."

Martha stood and carefully placed the heavy chair beneath the table. "Which reminds me... I need to see to their bedrooms. I gave the rooms a good airing, but I want to make sure everything is as it should be. They have been through so much...I am sure they are ready for a bit of rest." Martha patted Annabella's shoulder. "I am not sure I agree with your mother's solution, but remember that she loves you."

Annabella reached up and patted the calloused hand. "I will try."

Chapter Eleven

ANNABELLA PACED THE LENGTH of the parlor, her arms crossed with fingers tapping at the elbows of her bishop sleeves. Her face reddened and she blew up at a stray, red curl escaping her pompadour. Each step sent her flared skirt to swaying at her ankles. "I cannot believe that you think your plan is a viable option, Mama. What mother would deny her child?"

Agnes glanced at her sister, Lavinia, sitting next to her on the rose-colored, velvet sofa. "I think your mother is trying to find a solution to this difficult…situation we find ourselves in."

Lavinia sniffed, dabbing at her red nose with an embroidered handkerchief. "I have thought about this for several days now and I can think of no other way to handle this." She looked at her daughter. "You have shamed us, Annabella. Why do you not realize that?"

Annabella uncrossed her arms and made fists clenched at her sides. "I *do* realize that! I have thought of nothing else since it happened. But lying—"

"We are not lying to anyone!" Lavinia gripped the handkerchief into a ball of white and held it before her chest. "We are just not giving out information for people to gossip about. Your father founded this town, Annabella, and we have a reputation to uphold."

"You are always concerned with what people will think, rather than what is correct to do." Annabella walked to the long windows and pushed aside the lace curtains. "I would rather tell the truth."

"What is the truth, Annabella?" Agnes asked the question softly. "That you committed an act of indiscretion with a man that you were not sure you wanted to marry and then he died before you could *be* married and now you are with child?"

Annabella closed her eyes and sighed. "That sounds horrible."

"But *that* is the truth, Annabella," Agnes reminded her. "Dear Mr. Pratt is gone. He is with our Heavenly Father. Why do you want to smear his memory and good name?"

Annabella opened her eyes and laid her forehead against the molding of the window. "I do not want to ruin Thomas's reputation."

"Well, that is exactly what you will do if you tell the truth, my dear." Lavinia straightened her back and raised her chin. "No one knew that you were to marry Mr. Pratt. Even if they *had* known...you, you walking around, being huge with child, and not being married...well, it is unthinkable." She looked at Agnes. "My solution is the best. Annabella will remain in the house as her pregnancy progresses. She will have the baby here and we will let everyone know that she has adopted one of the children from a home in St. Louis. No one will think that is strange since you have been working with these children for so many years." She pointed toward the windows and the blonde-haired girl sitting on the porch swing. "Beth has traveled home with you every summer since she was practically an infant. Everyone in Rubyville thinks of her as your daughter, Annabella."

Agnes sighed. "That is a fact, Annabella."

Annabella dropped the curtain and turned to the sisters on the sofa. "We are speaking of my son or daughter...*my* child!" She gestured to her mother. "Your *grandchild*, Mama." She looked at her aunt. "Your niece or nephew. How can you ask it of me?"

"After what you have done, how can you not see that it is the best way to handle this?" Lavinia glared at her daughter, her brown eyes dark and unblinking.

Annabella crossed her arms once more. "So my child and I will pay the price of my indiscretion for the rest of our lives. Is that what you are saying?" Annabella met her mother's eyes and squared her chin.

"I am afraid so, Annabella. We all have a price to pay for bad decisions. There are consequences for our actions." Lavinia smoothed her plum and black striped skirt. "I have tried over and over to teach you this...but you have refused to learn."

Annabella looked at her aunt. "I cannot believe you think this is best, Aunt Agnes. You have seen what it does to a child to be denied their parents."

Agnes gave her niece a half-smile. "I have…but this will not be the same. Your child will know you as its mother. He or she will have family all around."

Lavinia shook her head in the negative, her small, brown curls shaking at the sides of her face. "I do not think that is best. For all our sakes, the child should believe they are adopted. You cannot expect a child to call you *Mama* while in the house and then remember you are not when out in public."

She shook her head again. "It will not work. For consistency sake, the child must know they are adopted…at least until they are older. If you wish to explain the situation when they reach adulthood…well that will be at your own discretion."

Agnes gaped at her sister. "You cannot mean that, Lavinia! You *are* asking Annabella to deny her own child!"

Lavinia took a deep breath and raised her chin higher. "If you choose to see it that way, then yes, I am asking that for now. I can see no other solution."

Annabella uncrossed her arms and clenched her fists once again, straightening her arms at her sides. "Then *I* will find another solution! I will not remain here in Rubyville with my own flesh and blood and *pretend* they are not of me!" She glanced between her mother and aunt. "I will search for Mr. Langworthy and beg him to take me back."

"Pregnant with another man's child?" Lavinia raised one brown, brow and snorted. "Why would he do that?"

"Because he said he loved me, Mama." Tears slipped from Annabella's green eyes. "Even after ten years he said he still loved me. He will take me back."

"You said he was with another woman…again. What if he perished in the tornado as well?" Lavinia spoke the words slowly.

Agnes cleared her throat. "Annabella, I had wanted to tell you, but I had not had a chance since I arrived yesterday." She gripped her hands in her lap. "Mr. Langworthy came to the house, just a few days before the tornado hit St. Louis. He said he was leaving on business again, but he wanted to speak with you since he only had a couple of days in the city."

She lowered her head. "I had just visited with Mr. Pratt and he was so happy, telling me that you had written and accepted his proposal of marriage. I informed Mr. Langworthy of the conversation."

Annabella gasped.

Agnes looked at her. "I thought he should know, Annabella. In all likelihood, you would have been married by the time he returned to St. Louis. I told him Mr. Pratt would be traveling with Beth and me to Rubyville so that you could be married."

Annabella dropped to the chair placed at the corner of the sofa. "What did he say?"

"He was distraught, telling me he had been trying to call on you for several weeks, but he had been traveling so much that he could not. He mentioned something about his sister-in-law being in St. Louis and wanting you to meet her." Agnes met Annabella's eyes. "It was difficult for me to understand everything that he was saying. He was talking so quickly—"

"But he knew I was to marry Mr. Pratt?" Annabella asked the question, her voice flat and low.

"Yes." Agnes looked at her niece. "I *am* sorry, Annabella."

"This is not of your doing, Agnes." Lavinia arranged her skirt and brushed at a stray piece of lint. "You have nothing to apologize for."

Annabella slumped in her chair, her face pale and drawn. "I guess I have no other options. I cannot live by myself and care for a child." She looked at Agnes, her green eyes brightening. "I could travel back with you, stay with you and continue on as we have been the past several years. It has worked very well for everyone…has it not?"

Agnes's brown eyes softened and brimmed with tears. "My dear Annabella, it has been wonderful to have you there in St. Louis with me. But as of right now, I have no home there. I do not know where I will be living. For now, I will be staying here in Rubyville. I think it best if we enroll Beth in school here. She has been through so much…seen so much for someone her age. She needs some stability right now…and she loves it here…she loves being with you."

Lavinia stood and straightened her skirt. "I am going to lie down for a bit. I have a dreadful headache coming on. All this excitement is more than I can handle." She glanced at her daughter, and then her sister. "I am happy that you both agree with me and see that it is for the best." She glided from the room, the rustle of her silk skirts, loud in the silence.

Agnes shook her head. "I would not say it is for the best." She watched as Lavinia climbed the stairs and disappeared into the upper rooms. "I have always known my sister to be fussy and rather selfish...not very concerned with those around her." She shook her head again. "But I have never thought her cruel until today."

Annabella leaned forward, resting her elbows on her knees as she buried her face in her hands. Sobs shook her shoulders.

Agnes slid from the sofa, kneeling at Annabella's feet. She wrapped her niece in her arms, rocking back and forth. "I will be here until the baby is born. We will get through this, Annabella. God will be watching over you and caring for you."

Annabella shook her head. "Not anymore...I have messed up my life too much for Him to care."

Agnes gripped her tighter. "That is nonsense and you know it. God does not go back on His Word. Luke chapter one, verse thirty-seven says that, *'for with God nothing shall be impossible.'* God keeps His promises...and there are so very many in the Bible. He promises to provide for our needs, which are shelter, food, and clothing. He has provided that here in Rubyville for you."

"Yes, but at what cost?" Annabella cried, great sobs shaking her body. "My child will never know me as a mother."

Agnes patted Annabella's back, smoothing the cotton fabric of her blouse. "Just concentrate on having a healthy baby right now. Thank the Lord for this child. Your mother will soften...you will see. She feels betrayed and angry right now...as though she has been a bad parent. Society turns their noses down on unmarried women having babies. Unfortunately, the women are blamed, not the men as well." Agnes smoothed back the stray hairs clinging to Annabella's wet cheeks. "And yes, this does happen in good Christian families. We have both seen it. We know that marriage is God's design and children are a blessing in it...but we are still human, and we do things wrong sometimes. God does not turn His back on us."

Annabella pulled back and looked at her aunt. "I am so thankful to have you here. I do not know what I would do without you."

Agnes smiled and wiped the tears from Annabella's face. "God has provided what you need. Always remember that you have two parents that love you *very* much. Your mother suffered greatly to bring children into this world…and she only has you. You are very important to her, Annabella, even if it does not seem like it at times. She has looked forward to having grandchildren for many years. I believe that there is a part of her that is thrilled to be a grandmother."

"I pray you are right, Aunt Agnes. I cannot bear the thought of not claiming my baby as my own."

Chapter Twelve

January 31, 1897
My beautiful daughter, Helen Barton was born on Sunday, January 24, 1897. The weather has been bitterly cold and miserable. Papa, Mama, Aunt Agnes, and Beth had just left for services that morning, bundled so that they could barely walk. Martha refused to attend. She said she could worship God and pray just as well from the comforts of her warm kitchen with a nice cup of hot tea! It was a good thing, too! My pains started late morning and Helen had arrived by four that afternoon. Mama said she had never heard of such a thing and that it was not natural to have a baby so easily. I am thankful that it was so.

There was a sound of movement from the cradle and Annabella closed her journal, tucking it into the drawer of her small desk. She walked softly to where Helen slept and looked down at her daughter. The pink, rosebud lips moved back and forth.

There was a knock at the partially closed bedroom door, followed by her father's head peeking in. "Is my beautiful granddaughter still asleep?"

Annabella smiled and waved her father in. "I am afraid so, but she will be up before long. She is starting to suck on her wrist."

William joined her at the cradle and gave her a side hug. "One week old today and the last day of the month as well." He shook his red head. "Where does the time go? It was only yesterday that you slept in that same cradle."

Annabella laughed. "No, Papa, it has been almost thirty-four years."

He gazed at her with feigned surprise. "Really?" He looked back at Helen. "She does not look at all like you, I am afraid. I see no sign of freckles or red hair. And that nose is not a Barton nose."

Annabella laughed. "She is a baby, Papa. I do not think many babies have freckles, and she is bald. She could have red hair." She crossed her arms. "She is definitely Thomas's daughter. She has his look and his nose. I think it would be lovely if she had blonde hair...I have never liked my red hair...or freckles." She gave her father a scowl. "Both of which I have you to thank for, may I remind you."

"Yes, you do, my dear." He gave her a nod. "But Helen is beautiful, just the way she is." He pulled his watch from his pocket and flipped it open. "Your mother sent me up to see if you felt well enough to join us for supper downstairs." He closed the gold timepiece and stuffed it back into the small pocket.

Annabella placed her hands at her slim hips. "I have felt well enough from the moment Helen was born. Mama was the one that banned me to my room for this past week."

William smiled. "I know, my dear. She just cannot seem to get past 'what should be' for a proper lady."

"I know, and I do try to be understanding of that. She is in a very different world than 1897. Why, she would faint if she knew I had ridden a bicycle in St. Louis and it was one that *Aunt Agnes* had purchased." Annabella smiled, her cheeks glowing.

William chuckled. "Please, do not convey that information."

Annabella reached out and patted her father's shoulder. "I will not, you can be assured. I do not know what I would have done all these months waiting for Helen to arrive if you and Aunt Agnes had not been here. Our midnight walks to the river until the weather turned were the highlight of my day. I also believe they helped in my quick recovery, but Mama would never agree with that."

William shook his head. "She would not. Having a baby is a sickness and women should stay off their feet and eat."

"Not very practical if you ask me."

"What is not practical?" Lavinia entered the room, slightly out of breath from her climbing of the stairs. She glanced at William. "I asked you to see if Annabella was well enough to join us in the dining room for our meal. Martha said she would make a tray if needed."

"I am feeling very well, Mama, and I accept your invitation with happiness. I do not like eating alone." Annabella gave her mother a smile. "I was thinking

Helen was waking to be fed, but she seems to have gone back to sleep."

"Well, one of us can come back up and get her if needed. Agnes and Beth seem to enjoy galloping up and down the stairs all day. You would think they would run all their errands at once and reduce the number of trips." She shook her brown head.

Just at that moment, Beth popped in. "Mama Bella, will you be coming downstairs? I asked for permission to eat here with you if you were staying in your room, but—"

Lavinia walked to Beth. "I told you to remain downstairs. We will continue working on your table manners. There is certain etiquette to the way a young lady conducts herself at the table. I am afraid you need much instruction in the area." Lavinia took Beth by the arm and directed her from the room. "I will be expecting you both shortly," she said, over her shoulder.

Father and daughter exchanged looks of sympathy for Beth as he held out his hand for her to go before him.

June 1897

BETH PUSHED THE WICKER baby carriage down the long drive leading from the Barton home. Helen giggled, her blue eyes taking in the fluttering leaves. Wisps of blonde hair peeked from beneath the white, organdy baby bonnet. Rosy pink cheeks on her porcelain skin made her resemble a doll.

Annabella laughed as she watched her daughter's enjoyment of the summer day. "Helen loves being outside. I cannot blame her. It was a long, cold winter."

"It was, but it was also fun. I loved going to the park and walking around Rubyville without all the crowds. Aunt Agnes says I must be a country girl." Beth smiled at Annabella.

"Did you enjoy school this past year? It must have been difficult to make new friends and get to know your teacher." Annabella brushed at one long red tendril escaping her upswept hair.

Beth frowned. "It was not really difficult, just different. I do miss

Melanie, but we write often. I miss Arthur and Ruth the most." She looked up at Annabella. "But they are so happy with their new family, I cannot be sad for them…just miss them." She shrugged her shoulders. "If I had my choice…I would live in Rubyville forever. I like my teacher and I will make new friends…but," she reached out and took Annabella's hand, "the most important thing is that I am with you."

Annabella's green eyes brimmed with tears. She let go of Beth's hand and put her arm around Beth's slight shoulders, hugging her to her side. "I never want us to part either. But I want you to be happy here, not just be here so you are near me. Aunt Agnes will be returning to St. Louis at the end of the summer. I want you to be sure that you wish to remain here with me. I know Mama can be difficult to bear at times." Annabella dropped her arm and walked alongside the baby carriage, straightening the light blanket across Helen's lap.

Beth laughed. "Yes, your mother is a trial and sometimes I wish to run and hide from all her rules. But you survived and became a great lady, and I can too. I have set my mind to it." She gave a firm nod of her head and looked back at the Barton home, growing smaller in the distance. "Mr. and Mrs. Barton have taken me in, and all of you have made me part of your family. I am very grateful for that. I have no family to call my own without you. So I will learn from Mrs. Barton and I will make you all proud one day."

"I am sure you will, dear Beth. I am sure you will."

They walked along in silence, the warm breeze fluttering the long sleeves of their blouses. Insects buzzed and birds hopped along, pecking for worms in the moist earth. They entered the park, the tall maples and oaks offering shade in the late morning sun. Across the park, children played, their laughter drifting through the town. On the west side of Rubyville, the large hotel took up most of a block, its whitewash exterior showing through the trees. Since its opening a few years before, it had been very successful with people stopping in Rubyville for a night or two and partaking of the country air. A restaurant business had begun the previous year. It was located on the bottom floor of the two-story building and it was talked about for miles around. Lavinia had even agreed to take a meal there once or twice and had admitted the fare was adequate.

Rubyville now boasted of two more churches: the Methodist church on the south side of the park and the newly built Catholic church on the block behind the hotel. The Barton Mercantile was located near the train depot. William Barton had designed it that way, knowing the easiest and most efficient way of keeping his store stocked was to be near the train. The middle-aged couple he had hired to run it several years before had become well-known in the area for their friendly service and excellent prices. The blacksmith and livery were also located near the train depot, on the south side of Rubyville, once more, the design of William Barton. He had wanted people to have easy accessibility to a horse and carriage when they traveled by train or have repairs made if needed.

They meandered through the park, nodding to others partaking of the late morning breeze and coolness before the afternoon heat began. They crossed the street in front of the Methodist church and turned east, walking out of Rubyville, toward the river.

Beth pointed to the tall, yellow house peeking from the cedars. "That is Mr. Langworthy's house…right?"

Annabella nodded. "Yes, it is."

"May we go look at it? I have always wanted to, but I did not think I should without permission." Beth's eyes sought Annabella's gaze.

Annabella paused and turned toward the house. "I do not see why not." She smoothed a hand down Beth's braid. "But you were correct to ask first. Someone's property is private and you should not trespass." She squinted through the trees. "I do not think Mr. Langworthy would mind. After all, he built it for him and me to live in."

Beth shook her head. "I do not understand what happened between you and Mr. Langworthy. We saw him that day with that woman…and then you never spoke with him again. Do you not miss him or wonder what he is doing?"

Annabella took the handle of the baby carriage. "I had better push this for now. The yard is overgrown and bumpy. We do not want Helen to take a tumble." She maneuvered the carriage through the cedars and stopped once they entered the large, front yard. The house stood tall and somehow lonely amongst the trees, the yellow paint starting to peel off the clapboard siding. The wicker furniture once placed around the long, front porch was now missing.

"Mr. Langworthy has not been here for a while, has he?" Beth stepped gingerly through the tall grass and walked up the front steps. She gestured for Annabella to follow. "Come on, we can rest here before we walk home."

"I am a bit nervous about snakes." Annabella surveyed the yard, her eyes darting here and there.

Beth shrugged. "I did not see any." She walked to the front door. "Maybe we can go inside."

Annabella scooped Helen from the carriage and lifted her walking skirt. "I am sure it is locked. Mr. Langworthy would not have left it open." She stepped swiftly through the grass, gaining the front porch in record time. She looked down at Helen who was watching her mother with round, blue eyes. "I do not know what I would have done if we came across a snake. It has been many years since your mama ran."

Helen gurgled at her.

Beth tried the door and frowned. "It *is* locked." She sighed and walked to each window along the front of the house, looking in. "It would have been so much fun to go inside." Beth turned back to Annabella and crossed her arms. "You did not answer my question. Do you miss Mr. Langworthy?"

Annabella took a seat on the peeling, white railing of the porch and settled Helen in her lap. "Of course I miss him. We were to be married at one time...and I thought we were again."

"But when you saw him that day with that pretty woman, you knew you could not marry him?"

Annabella took a deep breath. "That is correct."

"So then you thought you would marry Mr. Pratt after all?" Beth uncrossed her arms and walked to the railing, taking a seat at the tall column. Her blue eyes searched Annabella's face. "So who did you love, Mr. Langworthy or Mr. Pratt?"

Annabella looked away, her eyes seeking the yard beyond. "Beth, it is a very difficult situation. I do not think you would understand all that has transpired."

Beth crossed her arms once more. "I am no longer a baby. Why, I could marry in just a couple of years if I wished. Your mother married Mr. Barton when she was sixteen years old."

"Almost seventeen," Annabella corrected. "Besides, times are changing for women. No longer are they just expected to marry. They can further their education if they wish."

"I do not wish that. I would leave school now if I could." Beth set her chin and stared at Annabella.

"My point is that you are still young and you have your whole life ahead. Do not be in such a hurry. Let God direct you." Annabella adjusted Helen's bonnet and pulled her dress down over her chubby legs.

"I know all that, Mama Bella." Beth sighed and leaned back against the column. "I pray every day for God's direction in my life. But I know I want to marry and have children someday soon, maybe run a small business of my own."

Annabella's eyes lit up. "What kind of business would you like to have?"

Beth pursed her lips. "Martha has been showing me so much in the kitchen and I really enjoy it. I think I would like to have a place for people to eat. Martha said I am a quick learner and a good cook."

Annabella laughed. "You are a quick learner and people will always need to eat. I think you have a pretty sure business there."

Beth smiled, her pink cheeks glowing. "Mr. Barton said he could help me get started when the time came."

"That is wonderful, Beth! It sounds like you have your life all planned out."

Beth nodded. "I do…and that is why I want you to be happy too. You and your family have helped me so much. I do not want you to be sad."

Annabella looked away. "I am not sad. Why would you say a thing like that?"

"You are sad, I think you loved Mr. Langworthy and wanted to marry him. He built you such a nice house." She looked at the front windows, the heavy oak door and the intricate trim. "But I think you cared for Mr. Pratt as well. He is Helen's father, is he not?"

Annabella gasped and stared at the thirteen-year old girl. "You should not be talking of such…such intimate things at your age."

"Mama Bella, I spent a lot of time at the orphanage and I know what happened to Mary and her baby and I understand what my mother was. I am not as young as you believe." Beth held Annabella's gaze. "Aunt Agnes is always truthful and straightforward when I ask a question of her."

"And I am not?" Annabella asked the question softly, the hurt reflecting in her voice.

"You are most of the time…when it comes to other discussions we have. But you are not truthful about yourself."

Annabella looked away. "I do not know the best way to talk about what has happened over the past year or so. I want to be a good example to you…and Beth, I have not been." Tears brimmed and spilled over from her green eyes.

Beth stood and walked to Annabella, placing her arm around Annabella's shoulders. "You have been a great example of how to live my life, Mama Bella. You have taught me to love God, find direction in His Word, and to pray when I am struggling. You and Aunt Agnes have raised me as your own daughter and trained me to be a lady. I have so much more than I ever would have had living in the circumstances my own mother left me in." She squeezed Annabella to her side. "I only want to be there for you now and help you in any way I can. I know you are hurting. I know Helen belongs to you and Mr. Pratt, but I do not understand why it is to be kept a secret. The children at school think Helen is a baby you adopted from an orphanage in St. Louis."

"Have you told them otherwise?" Annabella pulled away and looked at Beth.

"No, because that is what your mother, Aunt Agnes, and you have said I should let people believe. But it is not true. I know Helen is your daughter."

Helen looked up at Beth and cooed.

Beth smiled at the baby and took her from Annabella's lap. Helen snuggled against Beth's shoulder and closed her eyes, blonde lashes laid against porcelain cheeks. "You are a sweetheart," Beth whispered against the bonnet.

Annabella watched the interaction between her daughter and the young woman she loved as a daughter. "You are correct, Beth. You are old enough to understand what has happened and why, and I most certainly owe you the truth. I would want nothing less from you." She sighed and rubbed her temples as she stood. She walked to the long window of the parlor and looked in. The room remained as she had designed it, the furniture placed where she had wanted it. The furniture was covered in dust, velvet chairs and sofa faded from the sun coming in the windows. She stood at the window and cried.

"I loved him so much and he hurt me greatly. I wanted everything to work out when I met him in St. Louis...and then he hurt me again. I went to Mr. Pratt. I knew he loved me and wanted to marry me. I used that information for wrong purposes...but I would have been a good wife to him." She sniffed and pressed the side of her hand to her nose. "But when Mr. Pratt came to the house, asked me to marry him, I felt so badly about what I had done with him and I wanted time to think about everything."

"So you came here." Beth said the words gently as she laid her cheek against the white bonnet of the sleeping baby.

Annabella nodded. "Yes, and after a few weeks, I wrote Mr. Pratt and let him know I would marry him." She closed her eyes. "But then the tornado hit St. Louis, and shortly after that I knew I was expecting Helen." Annabella cried, leaning her head against the peeling paint of the house. "I thought I could find Mr. Langworthy, but Aunt Agnes said she had talked with him and told him I was to marry Mr. Pratt...so then, so then he—"

"He was gone too." Beth walked over to Annabella and laid a hand on her arm. She stared into Annabella's green eyes. "But why would you say that Helen was not your baby? You could have said that your husband had died."

"Mama wanted it to be as it is. She said that no one knew I was to be married so I could not plead a husband, dead or alive." She sniffed again. "It is shameful to have a baby without being married and Mama did not want to face that here in Rubyville. Because I had done so many things in the wrong way, I agreed to go along with her plan...even though I did not want to."

"Is it not better to tell the truth, even if it causes shame?" Beth met Annabella's eyes with her own. "Helen needs to know you are her mother as she grows older. What does it matter if people know you did something wrong? We all do wrong things."

Annabella gave Beth a half-smile. "If it were just me being shamed, I would let the town know and live with the consequences. But I cannot ask that of my parents, or of Mr. Pratt's reputation, or even Helen. For now, I will go along with my mother's plan." She pushed away from the clapboard siding and reached out for Beth, enveloping her and the baby in a hug. She pulled back and looked at Beth. "And it is always best to tell the truth. The way may be rough for a while, but it will smooth out. Someday I will tell Helen the truth. Until then, I will love her as my daughter…and I ask that you will keep our secret until that day."

Chapter Thirteen

August 1900

A NOTHER SUMMER, COME AND gone…they seem to pass more quickly each year." Agnes slid her slight frame into the wicker chair opposite of Annabella's rocker. She took the fan from the small table beside the chairs and waved it before her face. "It has been so warm today. Lavinia is lying down with another one of her headaches. I think the heat makes them worse."

Annabella nodded. "I fear she is failing. She does not have the endurance she once had."

"The loss of so many babies took a toll on her health I am afraid. She never regained the vitality she once had." Agnes gestured to the sleeping infant in Annabella's arms. "That new grandson has been a delight to her this summer."

Annabella smiled down at the baby, adjusting his position in her arms. "He is a beautiful baby…so much curly, dark hair. I cannot imagine a mother leaving him on the doorstep of the church."

"That was much better than other areas we have found children. I am sure it was another instance of not being able to care for the child; too many other children at home or a single mother with no support from family." Agnes shook her head. "I have been doing this for so many years, and it still breaks my heart to see what is happening."

Annabella smiled. "I am just happy that you thought to bring little James here. He makes a wonderful addition to our family." She smoothed her hand down one thin, light brown leg. "We will have him in fine form before Christmas. With Martha's cooking and all our love, James will be hale and hearty in no time."

Agnes laughed and patted the beads of perspiration from her upper lip. "By the time I arrive next June, little Helen will be four years old and James over a year…walking everywhere I imagine. Beth will be engaged to her young man and probably planning a wedding." She shook her head and sighed. "The time spent away is becoming harder to bear. I am missing so much."

"You know Mama has asked you to come and live in Rubyville. She would love to have you nearby." James woke and started fussing. Annabella placed him on her shoulder and patted his tiny back. "I know…it is so very hot today. I thought the breeze would help." Annabella talked softly, comforting the baby.

"I *have* thought of selling the house in St. Louis. Our Papa purchased that house so many years ago. I have not wanted to sell it for that reason. After all the repairs from the tornado I thought I should just stay there, but it is much too big for me, living there alone. Mr. and Mrs. Jacobs have been with me for so many years and they do a lovely job taking care of the house and yard, but I know they would like to purchase a small place of their own and enjoy their later years." Agnes sighed and smoothed back the stray, gray hairs at her temple. "A nice, young family should be enjoying the house." She clasped her hands in lap. "I will pray about it over the winter…see what the Lord would have me to do."

"Mama, Mama!" called Helen as she broke from Beth's hand and ran the distance up the front walk to the wide stairs. She climbed them on short legs, a chubby hand placed on the stair ahead for assistance.

Annabella gently passed the sleeping James to Agnes and held her arms out for her daughter. "Where have you been, Sweetheart? Mama missed you, *so* much!"

The three-year old gained the porch and ran to her mother, throwing herself into the welcoming arms. "Beth and…and me." Helen paused to take a deep breath and brush at her sweaty forehead. Blonde hair was plastered to her red cheeks. "We was playing in the park. Beth…Beth said it was too hot…and…and we had to go home." She looked at Beth for confirmation.

Beth nodded and lifted the long length of her wavy, blonde hair off the back of her neck. "That is exactly what I said, Helen." She gave the little girl a smile. "But we had fun swinging for awhile, did we not?"

Helen giggled and shook her head up and down. She turned to her mother. "It was fun! Beth...she pushed me high...I almost touched the sky!" Helen looked back at Beth. "Did I almost touch the sky?"

Beth laughed. "Not quite, but you were high in the air. Almost like a bird."

"I want to be a bird. I like to be high in the air." Helen turned to her mother and placed her chubby hands on Annabella's arms. "Beth said, 'Hang on!' when I was up high." She reached one arm up and stretched her fingers.

"That is right, Sweetheart. It was good that you obeyed Beth so that you were not hurt." Annabella brushed the damp hair from Helen's face. "Now go into the kitchen. I think Martha has some lemonade for you and Beth. It will help you cool off a bit."

Beth held out her hand and Helen placed her hand in it. "I like lemon...lemon—"

"Lemonade," Beth supplied. "I like it, too. Martha's lemonade is the best. She might even have a sugar cookie for us."

Annabella smiled up at Beth. "Thank you, dear."

Beth returned the smile and led Helen around the porch to the kitchen door. Helen's chattering could be heard until the closing of the door.

"She is such a big help with Helen. And she loves being here in Rubyville. It was the correct decision to have her live here, with you." Agnes kissed the curly, black hair of the sleeping baby snuggled against her shoulder. "I am going to miss everyone so much."

Annabella reached out and patted Agnes's knee. "Remember, you are always welcome here. Rubyville has grown so much; you will not miss St. Louis at all."

Agnes's gaze followed the line of the trees along the river to the park, nestled in the shade of the hardwoods. "You just may be right. As I get older, a slower pace and country air seems to agree with me more and more."

October 1900

ANNABELLA CREPT DOWN THE hall by the light of the full moon. She paused outside of the partially closed door and listened. All was quiet…and then she heard the soft hum of a lullaby. She pushed the door open and stepped softly into the nursery, pulling her wrapper closed. "Mama, what are you doing up? It is two in the morning." She stopped beside the rocking chair that held her mother and James.

"I heard him fussing around midnight and I checked to see if he was alright. This room can be rather cold, as you know. October evenings can be chilly for such a little person." Lavinia tightened the blanket about James thin frame and pressed him close to her chest. "You know how much he likes to be cuddled. He will not abide by it for long. In no time at all he will be walking and not want to be held."

Annabella put a hand on her mother's shoulder. "I can sit with him, Mama. You need your rest. You know you have not been feeling well yourself."

"I am doing just fine, right now. There is nothing that you or Martha cannot see to tomorrow if I tire during the day. James needs me." She leaned down and pressed a kiss against the sleeping baby's cheek.

"Mama, I have been thinking that maybe we should ask Dr. Rundell to take a look at James."

"Whatever for? James is a perfectly healthy seven-month old. He *is* a bit small for his age, but he had a rough start." Lavinia hummed and rocked back and forth.

"Mama, he is not progressing as he should. It is difficult to get him to eat and he is very fussy for a baby his age." Annabella sighed and walked to the window. She looked down at the moonlit yard. Leaves scattered across the grass with each gust of cold wind. "I just think that Dr. Rundell may have some answers for us. I am at a loss as to what I should do."

"Well, he is your child and if you think it best that the doctor sees him, than that is your decision. But I think you are making more of a fuss then needs to be made. James needs a lot of love and security. Those are the best ways to heal anyone." She continued rocking and humming, talking softly to the baby.

DR. RUNDELL LAID JAMES in the crib and covered him with the blue knitted blanket lying at the foot of the crib. He turned to the group of people gathered in the nursery and smiled. "It is most unusual to have so many concerned faces when I do an exam."

Annabella clasped her hands. "I do apologize for the crowd, but James is very important to all of us and we have been worried about him. I just thought it would be best to have us all here, rather than relay the news to everyone."

Dr. Rundell chuckled and scratched his bushy beard. "It makes no difference to me. I am a country doctor for a reason. I do not adhere to all those fancy ways of the city."

Lavinia spoke from the rocking chair beside the crib. "James is just fine. I keep telling Annabella that she has nothing to worry about. It is just taking him a little longer to build his strength."

Dr. Rundell shook his head. "I have done a complete exam...or at least as much as I can do without running more tests. I cannot find anything physically wrong with the little man, but he is not thriving. He is not gaining weight and growing as he should. He also has delayed development in several areas."

"What does that mean exactly?" William walked over to where Lavinia sat and placed a hand on her shoulder. "He seems normal to me."

Dr. Rundell placed his stethoscope in the black bag setting on the blanket chest. "Well, at seven months, he should be sitting up, rolling over, maybe crawling. You have said he does none of those things." He looked at Annabella.

Annabella shook her head in the negative. "He will smile once in a while; hold your finger...activities of a baby a few months younger than what he is."

"Yes, I am seeing that." Dr. Rundell snapped his bag shut. "I can only surmise that he has something not functioning properly in his brain. Since he came to you when he was a couple months old, you do not know what took place in the first few weeks."

"My sister, Agnes, said he was found on a church doorstep when he was just a few hours old. He was taken to the children's home there in St. Louis and cared for until Annabella took him as her own." Lavinia gripped her hands together in her lap, watching the sleeping baby.

The doctor shook his head. "As I just stated, you do not know what took place before he was found. You do not know what condition the mother was in, if he was born early..." He sighed. "Too many unknowns." He took his black bag from the chest. "I will return next month to check on him. Just continue what you all are doing. Love him, care for him. I think that is why he is still here." He left the room, Annabella following him.

They took the stairs to the foyer. Annabella lifted the doctor's hat from the brass hook and handed it to him. "He is not going to make it, is he?"

The doctor looked at her and shook his head. "I pray I am wrong. I saw this too many times when I was a younger man in Kansas City. Children born under the circumstances such as James have many battles to survive. Very few do. You do not know what took place before he was found. I really do believe that the love and the care he has received here have prolonged his life."

Annabella bent her head, tears brimming over. "But it was not enough to save him."

Dr. Rundell cleared his throat and placed the hat on his gray head. "I will return next month." He opened the heavy door, the crisp autumn air floating into the foyer.

December 1900

ANNABELLA SAT ON THE edge of Helen's bed and tucked the covers around the little girl's dimpled chin. "I want you to stay nice and warm. It is cold out tonight." Annabella shook her finger at the three-year old. "No getting out of bed to scamper around the house like a little mouse."

Helen giggled. "I be good, Mama. I stay in bed." She wiggled her toes. "James stays in bed, too."

Annabella looked away and brushed at the tears spilling from her eyes. She cleared her throat and turned back to Helen. "Remember what Mama told you...James is in Heaven with God. God will take very good care of him and He will make sure James stays warm."

Helen nodded. "I be with God and James, too."

Annabella leaned down and pressed her daughter close. "Someday, Sweetheart... but not for many, many years. Mama needs you with her for now. I love you so much!"

Helen squirmed and giggled. "I love you! Is Santa Claus coming 'night?"

Annabella pushed back and smoothed the covers over Helen's tummy. "Not tonight, but soon. Just three more days and Santa Claus will be here. Have you been very good?" Annabella tapped Helen's nose.

Helen nodded. "*Very* good! Grammy says so."

Annabella smiled. "And Grammy is always right." Annabella sat up and clasped her hands in her lap. "Do you remember why we celebrate Christmas?"

Helen's blue eyes grew round. "Jesus was born...a baby in a manger. He is most 'portant part of Chistmas!"

Annabella leaned over and kissed Helen's forehead. "Yes, Jesus is the most important part of Christmas. We celebrate His birth." She sat up and stood beside the bed. "Now it is time for you to be sleeping. Mama will see you in the morning. I love you, Helen!"

"See you in morning! Love you!" Helen snuggled down in the bed and closed her eyes.

Annabella smiled, the tears flowing once more as she walked from the room, pulling the door almost closed behind her. Her eyes sought the closed door across the wide hall and she walked quickly to her bedroom, shutting the door.

Chapter Fourteen

WHAT A TREAT, MY favorite daughter and granddaughter coming to visit in the middle of the day." William gestured to the large napkin-covered basket swinging from Annabella's arm. "It looks as though you have brought provisions as well." He sniffed and closed his eyes. "I can smell Martha's fried chicken from here."

Annabella laughed and set the basket upon the large desk in the depot office. "Mama said you would not be home for dinner today since you would be covering for Mr. Norton."

William leaned back in the banker's chair and held his arms out for Helen. "We can have a little ride before we eat."

The four-year old giggled and ran to her grandfather, hopping into his lap. "I *like* to ride!" Helen stated, her blue eyes sparkling with anticipation.

William laughed. "I know you do! Grandpa rather enjoys it as well." He set Helen firmly on his lap. "Now, remember to hold tight."

Helen nodded, eyes jumping with glee, dimpled cheeks round and rosy. She grabbed the arm of the chair and looked up at William. "Ready!"

William grasped the little girl around the waist and used his feet to propel them across the long depot building. The wheels on the chair made a clunking sound as they rolled across the hardwood floor. As they gained momentum, William lifted his feet, coasting to the far wall. He stopped, and then spun the chair around before repeating the process. They glided back to where Annabella stood at the desk, unpacking the dinner.

Annabella laughed and shook her head. "You two are quite the pair."

William coasted to a stop in front of the desk. "What was that? I could not hear you over the sound of us having *fun*." William poked his granddaughter in the tummy and set her on the floor. "Your grandpa needs to take a rest. He is not as young as he used to be." He took a handkerchief from his pocket and wiped at his brow.

Helen leaned on the arm of the chair, one foot on top of the other and looked up at William. "You hot?" She frowned and watched as he wiped the handkerchief around his neck.

William leaned down and tapped her nose. "Yes, I am hot…too much exertion for a warm afternoon."

Helen reached up and brushed the blonde hair away from her face with both hands. "I'm hot too, just like you."

"It is a good thing that Martha packed some of her lemonade. That will help to cool you both." Annabella laid a napkin for each of them and placed a biscuit and piece of fried chicken on it. "There is even a slice of cake for each of us, leftover from last night's supper."

Helen clapped her hands.

"You have to eat all your dinner first, my dear." Annabella raised a brow and pulled up a chair to sit on.

William wiggled his brows at Helen, making her laugh. "I remember when your mother was not such a boring person." He grabbed Helen under the arms and sat her on his lap. "You can eat right here, just be sure to not dribble on me." He gave Helen a wink.

Helen shook her head. "I will not dibble on you."

William and Annabella exchanged smiles at the mispronounced word.

They bowed their heads as William prayed over their meal. "And dear Lord, please watch over my wife. Give her strength each day to do the things she needs to do and wants to do. I thank you for the time we have had together. In your precious Son's name…Amen."

Annabella took a sip of her lemonade. "Mama has had a good day so far."

William nodded his head. "I was pleased to see that she was able to come down for breakfast. Some days she is not able to."

"Yes, and she sat in the parlor for a while. She read to Helen—"

"She read about Noah!" Helen smiled up at William.

"Yes, dear, she did. But you should not interrupt when someone is talking, and especially when you have food in your mouth." Annabella took a chunk of chicken off the front of Helen's dress.

"Were there a lot of animals in the story about Noah?" William looked at his granddaughter.

Helen shook her head and held up two fingers. "Only two."

William frowned. "Only two animals in the story of Noah and the ark?" He shook his head. "I will have to speak with your grandmother about that."

Annabella laughed. "Helen, I think you mean that there were two animals of each kind."

Helen nodded and held up two fingers once more.

"I am surprised that Beth did not join you today." William took a bite of his biscuit.

"Believe me…if she thought she could have, she would have been here." Annabella shook her head. "I spoke with her just last night about the merits of staying in school for the last two weeks. She just does not see the need to be there if this is her last year and she will be married next month."

William helped Helen with her lemonade. "I do not think you need to worry about Beth. She has a good, strong head on her shoulders. She will do what is right. But you can understand her impatience to be going on with her life. She sees school as holding her back." William lowered his voice and met Annabella's gaze. "I know of another young lady who would have felt the same."

Annabella sighed. "I know, Papa. I never was much on sitting and learning."

William glanced up at the large, round clock on the wall. "The train will be in soon." He drained his glass and patted the napkin across his lips. He placed a kiss on the top of Helen's blonde head and set her on the floor. "I have a couple of items needing my attention out on the platform before the train arrives."

Annabella folded the crumbs into the napkins and placed the white balls into the basket. "Do not be lifting anything too heavy out there. You know how Mama worries about you on the days you fill in for Mr. Norton. You are not a young man anymore."

William scoffed as he shrugged into his sack coat. "I will be sixty-one this year, not ninety-one. Keeping busy is what keeps me young."

"Well, you can stay busy without hurting your back and putting yourself in bed for several weeks. Just please be careful." Annabella walked over and placed a kiss on her father's cheek.

William smiled down at his daughter. "I will, Bella. I have many years left on this old earth and I aim to enjoy them." He smoothed his hand down Helen's straight hair. "You be good too."

Helen smiled up at William and nodded.

HELEN SKIPPED ALONGSIDE HER mother, chattering like a disturbed squirrel in a tree. Annabella commented here and there as she enjoyed the late spring day. She shifted the basket to her right arm. "We should have ridden Misty over to the train depot. This basket is becoming a real burden to carry."

Helen slowed to a walk. "I *love* Misty!"

"I know you do, Sweetheart. Your grandpa should have given her to you rather than me. Then you both could have grown old together."

There will never be a replacement for Strawberry. We understood one another, just as Misty and Helen understand one another. Annabella smiled at the remembered words from Beth on that long ago day in January as they walked home. *'I know you are sad about your horse dying, but surely you can get another one. I will be praying that God sends another one to Rubyville for you. I think she should be white with a long, black mane and tail.'*

God gave me what you asked for, Beth. Misty is the palest white with a black mane and tail...she just is not Strawberry.

"I want to see Misty and pet her. Can I see Misty and pet her, Mama?" Helen looked up at Annabella, her eyes wide and round.

"I think Misty would enjoy a visit when we get home. Maybe Peter will have time to saddle her for us and we can take a little ride before supper." She looked down at Helen and gave her a smile. "Would you like that?"

Helen clapped her hands.

Annabella turned at the sound of a carriage coming up behind them. She grabbed Helen's hand and steered her to the sidewalk in front of the Methodist church.

"Annabella?" The carriage slowed and the masculine voice called again. "Annabella Barton!"

Annabella stopped and turned, narrowing her eyes as she tried to recognize the face shaded by the tall trees surrounding the park. The driver pulled the horse to a stop and laid the reins over the dashboard before jumping down. Annabella gasped and gripped Helen's hand tighter.

"Mama, that hurts," complained Helen, trying to wiggle her hand free.

Annabella let go and placed the hand at her lace-covered throat.

Orin glanced down at the little girl and his dark eyes found Annabella's green ones. "I *knew* it had to be you! What are you doing here in Rubyville? I thought you were in St. Louis with your husband."

Helen scowled up at the dark-haired man and then looked at her mother. "We live here." She tugged on a flounce of the lace overskirt Annabella wore. "I want to see Misty."

Annabella blinked and took Helen's hand, stopping the tug at her skirt. "Orin?"

Orin grinned, the graying mustache lifting at the corner. "Yes, Annabella...it is me." He swept his trilby hat from his dark head. "A little older... a little grayer...but me." His eyes swept the length of her lavender day dress and rested upon her pale face. "You are still just as beautiful as you always were."

Her face blushed red and she looked down at Helen. "This is my daughter, Helen. Helen, this is Mr. Langworthy. He is an old...friend of mine."

Orin set the hat upon his head and knelt before Helen, holding out his right hand. "It is very nice to meet you, Miss Helen."

Helen shook his hand and then backed against her mother, turning her face into her mother's skirts.

"I am sorry; she does not meet many new people." Annabella set the basket upon the sidewalk.

Orin glanced down at the red mark upon her forearm and reached out, gripping her elbow. He held her arm up, examining the indentation. "That looks a little heavy to be carrying. May I give you a ride to your destination?"

Annabella pulled her arm away and shook her head. "That will not be necessary. We do not have far to go." She bent to pick up the basket.

Orin swept it up from the sidewalk. He turned, placed it on the floor of the carriage and held his hand out to her. "I insist. It is too heavy and the day is hot." He looked north and gestured to the Barton home in the distance. "I assume that is where you are headed?"

Annabella nodded and placed her hand in his. She closed her eyes for a moment, relishing the warmth and strength of his hand. She opened her eyes and stepped into the carriage.

Orin leaned close to her and whispered, "I felt it as well." He turned to Helen and scooped her up, setting her upon Annabella's lap.

Chapter Fifteen

I CANNOT BELIEVE THAT you so boldly told my mother and Beth that you were taking me for a ride! Did you see the looks on their faces? When I get home I am going to have some explaining to do."

Annabella held her flat, wide bonnet with one hand and gripped the side of the carriage with the other. She looked down at her lavender dress, the light material fluttering in the breeze and lifting around her ankles. "I am not even properly dressed."

Orin turned to her and grinned. "You are beautiful and just as you should be. You are not a stuffy female, Annabella. Why do you try to play the part?"

Annabella focused on the line of cottonwood trees coming closer. "I am *not* playing a part. There are just some things that are appropriate and inappropriate, and being out with you, alone like this, is *not* appropriate." She shrieked as the carriage hit a hole and continued to bump along. "Why are you going so fast? I will not have a hair in place by the time you stop."

He grinned at her once again. "Good! I always wanted to see it down."

Annabella huffed and shook her head.

Orin slowed the horse to a walk, pulling on the right rein to guide it closer to the shade of the cottonwoods. Orin nodded to his left. "The soddy your father built is showing a little worse for wear."

Annabella looked at the four walls, the top layer of sod crumbling. "The roof caved in a couple of years back. Now the wind and rain are eating away at it. Before long it will just be a big pile of dirt." She gave a half-smile. "I spent many a summer day there, enjoying the coolness inside, and walking to the river to fish."

"That is where you went the day you left me at the altar." Orin gave her a sideways glance before guiding the horse into the trees and

117

stopping. The horse pulled at the reins and lowered its head to nibble at the tall grass along the river.

"How did you know that?" Annabella lifted a long, red tendril of hair off her shoulder and tried to tuck it into the bun atop her head. It fell down, bringing more with it. "Oh *bother!*"

Orin smiled, draping the reins over the dashboard. He leaned back against the leather tufted seat and braced one booted foot against the dashboard. "Your father told me you were hiding out at the soddy, dressed in your britches." He looked over at her, watching as she tried once more to pin up her hair. "You do remember that he came to speak with me that day?"

Annabella nodded. "Just as he should have."

Orin leaned his head back and looked at the leaves hanging over them. He squinted as a beam of sunlight slashed through the trees. "I never even had a chance to see you in your wedding finery."

Annabella looked over, her hair escaping the confines of the chignon hidden under the large hat. "Orin, why are you here? It cannot be to talk about a long ago wedding, that was never meant to happen."

He turned to her. "I almost believe you when you say that…that it was never meant to happen. But I know differently, Annabella. I know you regret it as much as I do."

She looked away, hoping the breeze would cool the heat she felt in her cheeks.

Orin took his foot off the dashboard and leaned forward, placing his elbows on his knees. He gripped his hands together. "I came to see to the house. I felt it was time to clean it out, get it ready to sell. With you being married," he glanced at her, "and now knowing you have a child as well, I see no point in keeping it any longer." He shook his head. "I saw your father when I got off the train. He did not tell me that you were here in Rubyville. I thought you were in St. Louis with your husband."

Annabella frowned. "You are going to sell our home?" The words were almost whispered.

Orin snorted as he looked over at her. "*Our* home? It was never *ours*, Annabella."

She reached up and tucked another strand of hair under the hat.

Orin grabbed the hat pin, pulled it from the hat and yanked the lavender confection from the tumbled, red hair. He tossed it in the back of the carriage. He pulled the hair pins from what was left of the bun and placed them in his vest pocket. "Now, will you quit messing with your hair and talk to me? I have not seen you for more than five years. I have some things I need to say."

Annabella gaped at him. "I cannot believe you did that. You are always doing things that are not appropriate…talking about things…things that should not be spoken of." She sputtered and spewed as she gathered the long length of hair and draped it across her shoulder to hang to her lap.

"When did you become a prude, Annabella?" Orin shook his head. "I think you have spent too much time here with your mother…Lavinia the Righteous. It may be time to return to your husband."

Annabella gasped and twisted to grip the side of the carriage. "I will not sit here and listen to you talk about my mother in such a disrespectful fashion! She has raised me to be a lady. God knows I have let her down many times in that regard." She threw her leg over the side of the carriage.

Orin grabbed her arm and drew her back to his side. "You are not going anywhere. You will sit here and listen to every last word I have to say. I will not be pushed aside and ignored again."

Annabella shrugged out of his arm and turned to him. "*You* pushed aside and ignored? That is what you did with *me*! I waited and waited for you, Orin…and you never returned!"

He scoffed at her. "You waited for me? *You* waited for *me*?" He raised a black brow. "How long, Annabella…a few days? Your little girl has to be about five years old. You had to have married practically the day I left St. Louis."

Annabella clenched her fists in her lap. "Stop saying that! I am not married…I was *never* married!"

"How can that be? Helen looks exactly like Thomas Pratt. He has to be her father." He stared at her until his dark eyes widened. He looked away and took off his trilby hat, throwing it to the back of the carriage. He ran his hands through his hair.

She laid her hand upon his arm. "You have to let me explain, Orin."

He turned to her, gritting his teeth and squaring his jaw. His dark eyes turned liquid. "Do you know how I have missed you? When your Aunt Agnes told me you were to be married…I thought I would die…I wished I would. I could not stand the thought of you being with him, spending your life with him. I wanted it to be me…it *should* have been me all those years ago!" He swallowed deeply. "Now… to hear that you were with him in that way and you never married!" He took her by the upper arms. "I *wished* he would die so I could be with you…and…and all this time you were not even *married!*"

"Please Orin, you are hurting me." Annabella looked at him, her own eyes brimming over at the pain she saw reflected in his.

He dropped her arms and stared at her. "You have been here in Rubyville all this time."

She nodded. "I came here after I saw you with that woman—"

Orin drew his brows together and shook his head. "What woman? You cannot blame this on me *again*, Annabella. I have been with no one…until just a few months ago."

"Beth and I were walking and we saw you come out of a hat shop with a dark-haired woman. She kissed you on the cheek… right there in front of everyone." Annabella narrowed her eyes at him. "Then you helped her into a carriage and she rode away."

Orin turned and jumped from the carriage. The horse jerked its head up, its brown ears twitching back and forth, and watched as Orin paced beside the carriage. The horse shook its head and snorted before going back to the grass.

"That *woman* was my sister-in-law, Laura. She is *married* to Clint." He shoved his hand through his hair. "His first wife died in childbirth many years ago. I wanted you to meet her, I thought you both would be as sisters…you are so alike." His voice lowered at the last.

Annabella scooted to the side of the carriage and looked down at Orin. "I had no idea. I just thought you were acting the same way as you had before. I should have trusted you."

Orin walked to the side of the carriage and gripped the edge. He slowly raised his head and stared at her. "Yes, Annabella…you *should* have!"

Annabella sat back against the leather seat and slumped as she bowed her head. She clasped her hands in her lap. "I…I went to Thomas after I saw you with—"

"My *sister-in-law?*" He dropped his hands to his side and clenched his fists.

Annabella nodded. "I just threw myself at him…wanting him to feel guilty and marry me. Then when he asked to marry me again, I could not go through with it. I felt so terrible for using him like that. I came here to make a decision…but by the time I had decided to marry Thomas and…and we were making plans…" Her shoulders shook. "The tornado hit St. Louis and he was killed." The tears brimmed over and slid down her face, landing on the lavender lap and dotting it with purple. "Then… then I knew I was expecting Helen. I wanted to find you and beg you to take me back…but…but Aunt Agnes said she had told you I was to be married."

Orin climbed into the carriage and took Annabella into his arms. "I would have married you even then, my dearest. I loved you so much. I could not bear to think of my life without you again, after finding you."

Annabella laid her head against his chest. "We have spent so many years," she sniffed loudly, "chasing each other around in circles."

Orin lowered his head and kissed the top of her head. He smoothed his hand down her back, along the red hair. "Your hair is like silk beneath my fingers. Oh Annabella…what have we done?" He groaned and gripped her arms, pushing her away. He looked into her liquid green eyes. "I still love you…after all this time…I *still do.*" He looked away and let his hands slide the length of her arms.

She wiped the tears from her cheeks. "You said you had not been with anyone…until…until a few months ago." She brushed his arm. "What does that mean, Orin?"

He faced her. "I met someone at the beginning of the year. She is a younger woman, a very nice woman…and I have asked her to be my wife." He placed a hand against her cheek. "If I had known you never married, I would have found you. If I had known Thomas Pratt had died all those years ago, I would have contacted your parents, your aunt…anyone I could think of to find you, and marry you." He moved his thumb over her lips. "I love you so much, Annabella."

She moved toward him and placed her hands against his jaw line. "Then do not marry this other woman, Orin. Tell her you have changed your mind…that it will not work."

He took her wrists in his hands and gently laid them in her lap as he looked away. He narrowed his eyes at the western sun. "She is a good woman, Annabella. She is a Believer and she has taught me so much about living the Christian life, honoring God, just by her example in her own life. She also loves to travel. I have to do so much of it, as you know. I think we could build a life together." He turned back to her. "You and I have tried so many times to make it work. Maybe that is not God's plan for us."

Annabella scoffed. "*You* are talking about God's plan for your life? Since when was that a priority for you?"

"You have known that I was a Believer since the first day we met. Your father was the one that invited me to church, if you recall."

"Going to church does not save you." She arched one red brow at him.

"No, it does not." He rubbed the back of his neck. "I will admit that I attended church all those years ago to make a good impression on you and your parents. But I had already accepted Christ as my Savior. I also understand that I have not lived my life as a very good testimony to Him." He looked at her. "God always came second or third in my life. *Always* after my work and whatever free time I had to spend. I have come to know that is incorrect. God should be first in all that I do."

Annabella crossed her arms. "Well, I suppose this *young* woman you have asked to marry you has enlightened you…after all these years."

He nodded. "I would say that is true." He leaned back and looked up through the leaves. "When I lost you again…heard that you were marrying Thomas Pratt…I did not want to go on with my life, Annabella. I had never felt that way before. I could not bear the thought of waking up to a day without you in it." He dropped his head, one lock of hair falling across his forehead. "I also knew I did not want to become cynical as I had before when you left me. So, I started reading my Bible and attending services on Sunday mornings." He gave her a sideways glance. "It really helped me to start thinking about someone other than myself or..." he half-smiled, his mustache lifting at one corner, "you."

Annabella blushed and looked away. "If you care about someone, I think it is only natural that you think about them."

"I would agree with that, but you were all-consuming." He swept back the lock of hair. "For some reason, the relationship between you and I has always been that way. It has been like a fire that we cannot extinguish." He captured her eyes with his own. "I know you have felt it too." His dark depths pulled her in. "We feel it now."

Annabella cleared her throat and fought against the desire to fall into him. *Yes, Orin, it is there, just as it always has been with you...just as it never was with Thomas.* "What...what should we do about it?"

Orin lifted a tendril of hair from her shoulder and smoothed it between his thumb and forefinger. "I have just spent another five years trying to forget you. I came to Rubyville to clean out the house, sell it, and get on with my life." He placed a finger beneath her chin and turned her face to him. He leaned over and pressed his lips against hers.

Annabella closed her eyes at the exquisite pressure, the warmth spreading through her. She sighed deeply and sank against his strong chest. *You feel as though I am coming home, Orin. Everything is right in the world when I am with you.*

Orin gripped her shoulders and pushed her back against the leather seat as he broke away from her. His dark gaze searched her eyes, his face inches from hers. "I love you, Annabella Barton and I always will...which is why I am going to let you go."

Annabella gasped, her eyes widening. "You cannot kiss me like that and then speak those words to me."

He placed a finger before his lips. "Please let me finish. Whatever is between us, will destroy us. It is too much to conquer—"

"That is perfectly ridiculous! Why I have never—"

He raised his finger again, his breath warm against her face. "Maybe we are too much alike; too opinionated, headstrong, arrogant, call it

123

what you will. But it is time to move on and heal." His eyes swept her face, lingering on her lips. He closed his eyes and sat back. "Sarah is the woman I will spend the rest of my life with. I have asked her to marry me and I will have the integrity to see it through. She deserves nothing less from me."

"But you said you still loved *me*, Orin! Does that not make a difference? We have loved one another for so many years! You cannot give it up now, not after all that we have been through! If this Sarah is as wonderful as you say, she will understand and let you go. She will not want to be married to someone that loves another." Annabella gripped the sleeve of his sack coat.

"Sarah lost her entire family in that tornado in 1896. She has no one."

"So, you are marrying her out of a sense of guilt and wanting to take care of someone." Annabella crossed her arms once again. "That sounds very similar to the reasons I gave you for marrying Thomas all those years ago." She looked at him. "You laughed at me for that…remember?"

He nodded his dark head. "I do remember, but I also now understand." He leaned forward and ran his finger along the dashboard. "Sarah is young and beautiful, but what I admire the most about her is her giving and loyal heart. She loves God and wants to serve Him in everything she does and that overflows to everyone around her. It humbles me that she has agreed to be part of my life and she is willing to share that with me. I am not deserving of that." He glanced back at Annabella. "What makes it even more special is that she is blind, Annabella, and has been since birth."

Annabella put a hand to her mouth. "I am so sorry, Orin."

He smiled. "Do not feel sorry for her, my dear. She sees more clearly than either one of us ever will." He reached into the back of the carriage and picked up his trilby, placing it upon his head. He repeated the process and handed Annabella her bonnet. "We should be headed back. It will be supper time soon."

Annabella took the hat and laid it on her lap. "So that is it? You bring me out here," she gestured beyond the carriage, "to where we spent so much time together. Make me a wreck emotionally and otherwise, tell me you love me, kiss me, and then say you are going to marry another woman." She gaped at him and shook her head.

"I think that pretty well sums it up." He took the reins from the dashboard and clicked his tongue. He gently pulled on the left rein and steered the horse from the shade of the cottonwoods.

Chapter Sixteen

ANNABELLA REACHED FOR THE newel post and gathered the lavender skirt with her other hand as she set her foot on the bottom step.

"Annabella Barton, please come here this very instant," Lavinia called from the parlor.

Annabella sighed and retraced her steps across the foyer. She went to the arched door leading into the parlor and stood, her tousled hair hanging to her waist, the wide hat sitting crazily atop her head. "Yes, Mama…did you need something?"

Lavinia put a hand to her ruffled chest and looked her daughter up and down. "I thought I heard you coming in the front door. Whatever happened? You look as though you have been dragged behind the carriage." She sat up from her reclining position on the velvet sofa, pulling the knitted blanket across her lap.

Annabella pulled the hat from her head and slapped it against her leg. "It has been a very trying afternoon, Mama. May I repair my hair and wash up a bit before I talk with you?"

Lavinia shook her head. "Absolutely not! That Mr. Langworthy states that he is going to take you for a ride and you come back looking like a harridan. You need to explain what has been going on and what took so long." Lavinia's eyes swept her daughter once more. "He did not take advantage of you…did he?"

"*No*, he did not. It seems that Mr. Langworthy is now engaged to be married to some woman named Sarah. An upright, upstanding paragon of the community that is young and beautiful as well." She walked to the sofa and dropped to the tufted seat. "All the things that I am not."

Lavinia tsked-tsked, "If you looked like that the entire outing, it is no wonder. I have told you time and time again, Annabella that you have to be a lady. Men will—"

"Never want to marry someone that looks and acts like me. I know, Mama, you have told me so for thirty-eight years now. Beth has heard it, as well." She threw her hands up. "It seems that she listened to you since she will be married next month to a successful young man."

Lavinia sighed deeply and pulled at the blanket. "I do not think I have worded it in such a manner."

Annabella placed her hand over her mother's frail, bird-like hand. "I am sorry, Mama. This is why I did not want to speak with you right now. I am in a bad mood and I want to take it out on someone. I know that is not right, but I am *so* hurt and angry." She squeezed her mother's hand. "Why do I have to spend my life alone?"

"You have your father and I, and Martha. Beth is like a daughter to you and you have Helen."

"Who I cannot acknowledge as my own daughter." Her eyes flitted around the room, "Not outside these walls anyway." She looked at her mother. "Do you know that Mr. Langworthy recognized Helen as Mr. Pratt's daughter? He said they looked exactly alike."

Lavinia widened her eyes. "Well, that is exactly what I have been talking about all these years. You needed to stay in Rubyville so Helen would not be recognized. It would have ruined Mr. Pratt's reputation, as well as yours."

Annabella shook her head. "What difference does it make, Mama? Does anyone really care? Or is it just a bit of gossip for awhile until a new bit of juicy information comes along?"

Lavinia gasped. "I cannot believe you would say such a thing! Of course it matters!"

Annabella let go of her mother's hand and stood. "Well, I know it matters to you, which is why I have respected your decision all these years and lived a lie in this community." She walked to the arched doorway. "I just do not know if I can continue it much longer. I do not see the point...and after this afternoon's ride, I do not have much else to lose."

"Annabella, you cannot mean that! Annabella, you come back here and discuss this!" Lavinia's raised voice was lost to Annabella as she ran up the stairs to her bedroom.

THE MID-MORNING SUN BEAT down upon the sidewalk as Annabella exited the limestone bank. She shaded her eyes with her gloved hand and looked both ways on the dirt street before crossing. She entered the shade of the park and smiled at the children playing on the grass. Their laughter floated through the trees.

"Good morning, Miss Barton!" called a brown-haired boy. When he had Annabella's attention, he kicked the leather soccer ball across the corner of the park to another boy. "Mr. Barton gave this to us this morning. He said it just arrived on the train…he had ordered it…and we can use it in the park."

Annabella walked over and placed one hand upon her hip, watching the boys kick the ball back and forth. "That looks like a lot of fun. Might I give it a try?"

"Well sure, Miss Barton!" The brown-haired boy ran over with a grin on his face. He placed the ball on the grass. You just give it a kick, like this." He held his foot out and demonstrated. "That is what your father said."

Annabella set her packages on the ground and then hitched up her skirt. She held her foot to the side and kicked the ball with the inside of her foot, sending it flying across the park. She laughed. "How was that?"

He grinned up at her. "That was terrific…especially for your first time. I never saw no girl kick like that before." He wiped his arm across his forehead. "Do you want to kick a few more times?"

Annabella laughed. "No thank you. I just wanted to give it a try. You boys are doing a great job. I think I may sit in the gazebo and watch you for a bit, if that is alright."

"That's just fine, Miss Barton." He grinned and gave her a wave as he ran back to his corner.

"You never cease to amaze me, my dear."

Annabella turned and glanced up and down. "Have you taken to following me now? I would have thought you would be busy emptying the house and getting back to your intended."

Orin chuckled. "I had a few errands to run…and spoke with your father over at the Mercantile. I was on my way home when I saw you playing in the park." He gave her a wide smile, his white teeth a striking contrast to his dark mustache.

Annabella bent down and retrieved her packages. "I was not *playing in the park*. I just wanted to see if I could do it." She spun around and headed toward the gazebo.

"Might I carry those for you?" He walked alongside her, meeting her stride for stride.

"No, I am fine. I walk into Rubyville almost every day for some errand for either Mama or Martha. I am used to it." She glanced at him. "Besides, you do not have time to be helping me."

Orin took her elbow, stopping her progress across the park. "Annabella, can we not be friends? I still care for you and I have always enjoyed conversing with you."

"Orin, you cannot have everything your way." She shrugged at his hand. "You have made your decision. Now you need to leave me alone. Goodness knows I have spent years trying to forget you." She pressed her lips together and took a deep breath. "This time I will make sure I am successful." She proceeded through the park, passing the gazebo.

"You told those boys you were going to watch them play." Orin walked to the small, white building and climbed the steps.

"Well, I am certainly *not* going to sit there with you, Orin Langworthy. That would not be proper." She stopped and held her packages against her chest.

He shook his head and chuckled as he gestured around the grassy, shaded block. "We are right here, in the middle of the park. You may sit on one side and I will sit on the other. That way we will keep the tongues from wagging." He sat down on the wood bench encircling the inside of the gingerbread-trimmed building. "I need to talk with you anyway. As I said, I just spoke with your father and I wanted to get your opinion on it as well. It concerns Beth and her young man, Daniel."

"If you insist." She retraced her steps. "You have to make it quick. It will be time for dinner." She climbed the stairs and walked to the opposite side of the structure from where he sat. She set down her packages and took a seat, arranging her dark skirt across her lap. She folded her hands and looked at him. "Well?"

He took off his hat and laid it on the bench. "I was considering what you said about selling the house." He turned and braced one elbow along the top of the railing, his finger smoothing his mustache. "It has many memories for me. We did design it together, with the plan to live in it and raise a family."

Annabella crossed her arms and looked in the direction of the house he was speaking of. "Yes, we did. It holds many memories for me as well."

"You chose most of the furniture, rugs and draperies. Even after so many years, they are in good shape." He turned toward her and braced his elbows upon his knees. "I would like to offer the house and the furnishings to Beth and Daniel as a wedding gift, with the stipulation that if they wish to leave Rubyville, they return the house to me."

Annabella let her arms fall back to her lap. "That is very generous of you, Orin. But I really do not think they mind living at the hotel as they have planned. After all, Daniel has been living there for over a year now, every since he came here to manage it. Beth works in the kitchen several days a week. I think it is very convenient for them."

Orin waved his hand. "I know all that." He lowered his head. "I also know how much Rubyville means to Beth. You have raised her as your daughter. It would be almost as if one of our children was inheriting the house. That would mean a lot to me, Annabella. I would rather know that Beth and her Daniel are living there raising a family, than thinking about someone else being there." He raised his head and looked at her across the expanse of the gazebo. "Does that make any sense?"

Annabella closed her eyes and pressed her hand to her nose. "Yes…it does, Orin. It would make me very happy to know Beth is living there." Her eyes met his. "It *is* a very generous gift."

He sat back and cleared his throat. "I am happy that you understand." He looked away, the breeze lifting the dark layers of his hair. "This town will always hold a special place in my heart. I will always remember our rides through the tall, Kansas grass, our conversations about all sorts of topics. Now I will know that the house we built together will be loved and cared for, just as we designed it to be. It will be a home for a family." He turned back to her, his dark eyes intense and liquid. "I *do* love you, Annabella. I will always love you. Somehow, I know that will continue down through the generations to follow us. I have to believe that."

Annabella smoothed the tears from her cheeks. "I do not understand why we cannot be together…but I know it is true. You will always be a part of me, Orin…a part of Rubyville. Years from now, others will know that too." She bent her head. "I wish I could say I was happy for you and Sarah…but I cannot. Not now, but maybe in time. God only knows why our lives have worked out the way they have."

He smiled. "God only knows."

"I NOW PRESENT TO you, Mr. and Mrs. Daniel Johnson." The pastor smiled as he closed his Bible and held it at his side.

The beaming bride and groom turned to those gathered to witness their marriage ceremony. Beth's blue eyes sought Annabella, sitting on the front pew, and she smiled at the woman she had loved as a mother.

The couple walked down the aisle of the church, their hands entwined. Beth's ivory silk gown flowed into frothy lace layers upon the gleaming wood floor. The pink peonies, in a coronet atop her blonde hair, held a long trail of netting. Ivory satin slippers peaked beneath the wide hem with each step. The young couple walked through the foyer and stood at the double doors of the church, the morning sun illuminating their silhouettes. They laughed and waved at the gathering of people in the church yard, overflowing into the street.

"May I introduce you to my wife, Mrs. Daniel Johnson?" Daniel grinned and placed a kiss upon Beth's rosy cheek. "Today she is the most beautiful woman in Rubyville *and* the best cook."

Beth laughed heartily, her cheeks reddening even more.

Daniel pointed to the park. "You are all invited for the meal. I know many hands have helped to prepare it. We want you all to share in this day with us."

There was a loud sound of affirmation from the crowd and clapping of hands as they turned and walked to the park, children skipping alongside their parents.

Helen stood beside Beth in her flower girl finery and tugged on the lace dripping from Beth's sleeve. "May I sit with you and Dan?"

Beth knelt down and looked Helen eye to eye. "Of course you may. You are my favorite sister, after all."

Helen wrapped her arms around Beth's neck. "Thank you!"

Beth stood and held out her white-gloved hand to Helen as the threesome stepped down the stairs of the church. The church emptied behind them, the palest colors of summer displayed on the women's dresses.

Annabella stood in the foyer of the church and watched as her father and Agnes walked with her mother, each supporting an elbow as they traversed the street and made their way to the gaily decorated park.

"You are a beautiful mother-of-the-bride, if I may say so," Orin whispered soft and low as he stood behind her.

Annabella turned and smiled. "Thank you, Mr. Langworthy. You are fairly dashing yourself." Her eyes swept over the black morning coat and white shirt.

She turned back to the scene in the park. Long tables draped in white, fairly groaning with food. Families sat upon blankets, eating fried chicken, potato salad, and sandwiches made of ham. Women had opened their pantries to share pickles and fresh produce from their gardens. Another table was set with pies and cakes to go along with the white wedding cake Martha had made for the bride and groom. It sat upon a lace-draped table in the white gazebo, the three tiers peeking above the railing. The white frosting shimmered in the sunlight.

"When does your train leave?" Annabella's fingers adjusted the narrow belt at her waist. It was made in a slightly darker hue than her mulberry-colored gown, with ecru-colored lace edging the billowy elbow-length sleeves.

"In about two hours. I already have my baggage down at the depot."

Annabella wrapped her arms about her waist. "I am happy that you agreed to stay for Beth's wedding. I know she appreciated it, as well."

"I would not have missed it." Orin cleared his throat. "Beth agreed to write after she and Daniel are settled into the house. She wanted to let me know of everything they had planned. I enjoy seeing her excitement about it. I know they will have many happy years there."

Annabella nodded. "I believe they will, as well."

Orin held out his hand and opened it to show a small pile of hair pins. "I found these in my vest pocket when I was packing this morning. I thought you might need them."

Annabella looked up at his twinkling dark eyes. "I have plenty. I always seem to be misplacing them. I would not have remembered that you had them." She held out her hand, palm up.

He gave a half-smile and brushed her cheek with one finger, before transferring the pins to her hand. He closed her fingers around them and gripped her hand with both of his. "The memory of you, your hair hanging to your waist in all its red glory, will be with me forever." He bent down and placed a kiss upon her cheek. "I pray you have a good life, Annabella. I have instructed Beth to contact me if you ever need anything." He stood, straight and tall, gripping the lapels of the morning coat. He captured her eyes with his own, seeming to tear at her very soul. He turned and swept his top hat from the foyer table and placed it upon his dark head. He took the steps to the sidewalk, his long stride making short work of the distance to the edge of the park.

Annabella stood in the doorway until his form disappeared into the trees at the edge of his property, the tears flowing freely. She turned and walked back into the church and sat down on the last row of pews. Her eyes took in the vases of peonies and roses arranged at the front of the church and the rows of pews draped with pink fabric. Her mind flew back to that May in 1886... *fifteen years ago! This scene could be from our own wedding, Orin.* Annabella sat forward and leaned her arms on the pew in front of her. She placed her forehead there...and cried.

Chapter Seventeen

February 1902

B ETH CARRIED THE TRAY of tea into the parlor and set it on
the marble-topped table between the two rosewood chairs. She
glanced at Annabella, standing before the tall, turreted windows of the
parlor in the Barton home, her arms wrapped about her waist. The
black, bombazine dress she wore emphasized the slimness of her figure.

"Come, Mama Bella, it is warmer by the fire. A nice cup of hot tea
always makes you feel better." Beth walked to where Annabella stood
and leaned her blonde head against Annabella's thin shoulder as she slid
an arm about her waist. "Helen is helping Martha with cookies. We can
have a nice, long visit. I have some good news to share as well."

Annabella reached up and patted Beth's cheek. "Some good news
would be most welcome. We have had that in short supply, as of late."

Beth walked with Annabella to the pair of chairs and waited as she
sat down. Annabella arranged her black skirt as Beth poured the tea. She
handed Annabella a cup and saucer and gestured to the cookie on the
saucer. "That cookie is from the first batch, so it is still warm as well."

Annabella smiled and took a sip of tea. "I have missed being spoiled
by you. But I know Daniel is benefitting from it now."

Beth laughed and sat down on the tufted velvet cushion. She pulled
at the long, tight-fitting sleeves of her purple dress and laid her hands in
her lap. "I *love* taking care of him. He is so easy to please. Anything I do
is just fine with him."

Annabella took another sip and then placed her cup and saucer on
the table. "I pray it remains so for all the years of your marriage." She
gave Beth a wink. "I have heard that may change over the years."

Beth laughed and took a cookie from the plate. "Oh, I am sure it will, but I am really enjoying it right now."

Annabella looked down at the hands in her lap. "Have you remained in contact with Mr. Langworthy concerning the house?"

Beth looked at Annabella. "I will tell you all the news I know and then we will not speak any more of it. I know how it makes you sad, and I do not want to see you sad any longer."

"I really am trying to be happier, at least for Helen's sake, but it has been a difficult few months. I think Papa is faring better than I am."

"I know he misses your mother, but she was so very sick there at the end, that I think he was relieved to see her go home and be with her Heavenly Father. He knows she is in a better place."

Annabella nodded, the tears slipping down her cheeks. "I know Mama is better off where she is." She looked around the room. "But this house is so empty without her. I keep hearing her voice running through my head whenever I make a decision...even if it is as simple as what to wear for the day. She had such a presence here."

Beth smiled. "I understand...so much of what I know about being a lady is due to your mother. You and Aunt Agnes have taught me many things as well, but decorum was definitely your mother's forte."

Annabella gave a light laugh. "Just listen to the words you use. You *are* my mother's protégé."

Beth nodded. "I really am. All these years, I learned everything I could from her on how to be a great lady, just as she was." She looked over at Annabella. "Just as you are."

Annabella shook her head. "I will never be that, I am afraid. My mother tried, but she was not successful. I am very happy that she had you and then Helen. You were much better students than I ever was."

"I do wish Aunt Agnes had stayed for Thanksgiving and Christmas. It would have made them easier to bear without your mother. I was very disappointed that she returned to St. Louis." Beth took another cookie from the plate and nibbled on it.

Annabella sighed. "I know she wanted to return before the holidays and the bad weather set in. But she will be selling the house, now that mother is gone. If that goes well, I pray she will be here for good by the start of summer."

Beth smiled, her blue eyes twinkling as she sat forward in her chair. "That would be wonderful! Then she will be here when the baby arrives!"

Annabella gripped the arms of her chair. "Baby...are you expecting a baby?"

Beth nodded, the curls framing her face bouncing merrily. "I *am*! Dr. Rundell says sometime around the middle of September. Daniel is almost beside himself with excitement." She laughed. "He wanted to let everyone at the restaurant know, but I said I wanted to tell my family first." She patted her tummy. "It is also a little early yet. I want to wait a bit before all of Rubyville knows about it."

Annabella reached out her hand. Beth took it and they gripped tightly. "I am so very happy for you and Daniel. You need to fill that house with children. Those old walls need to hear children's laughter."

Beth smiled, her cheeks rosy and round. "I hope we will. I have always wanted a *huge* family." She squeezed Annabella's hand. "Just think, you and Aunt Agnes are going to be grandmothers."

"I *really* love the sound of that, my dearest Beth. You have brought so much joy into our lives over the years."

"Believe me, Mama Bella...I thank God every day for Aunt Agnes and you coming to see me at the children's home and then taking me to live with you. God provided me with a family...not in the conventional way that everyone thinks of, but He did." She gripped Annabella's hand with both of her hands. "He is *good*, Mama Bella...so good to us, whether we deserve it or not."

'HE IS GOOD, *MAMA Bella...so good to us whether we deserve it or not.'* Annabella laid her hand against her tummy, remembering the emotions when she was expecting Helen. *Now there will be another baby in the family, Father...a baby that will be loved by two parents and claimed as their own.* Beth's words repeated again. *Yes, Father, You have been good to me. You have seen me through so many bad decisions and difficult times...many of my own making. You*

gave me parents that loved me and cared for me. They taught me about You and lived a life of Your Son's example. They took me in when most parents would have set me aside for my actions.

She sighed and rolled over in her big bed, placing one hand beneath her cheek. Through the darkness, her eyes found the windows, silvery light glowing through the lace curtains. The world was quiet beyond the house, snowflakes drifting to the ground. *There is a different kind of quiet when it snows. It is as if even the animals know they are to seek shelter and remain hushed until the sun shines again.* She smiled at the memory of Helen's excitement about the snow. *Please send a lot of it, Father...or we will have a very disappointed five-year old in the morning.*

Annabella pulled up the heavy quilt, tucking it around her chin. The tall clock in the hallway chimed three times, and was silent. *Not much night left to sleep.* Her thoughts raced back to the conversation with Beth that afternoon when she was leaving. She had reminded Beth that she had not followed up on what she had said about sharing news from Mr. Langworthy.

Beth had shaken her head as she buttoned up her long, wool coat. "I was hoping that you would forget." She had placed the matching hat upon her head, securing it over her blonde, upswept curls. "Mr. Langworthy wrote a few weeks ago...around the first of the year. He said he had been married in October and that they were residing in St. Louis through the winter. He was expecting his work to take him to the East for a period of a couple years. He asked after the house and wanted me to send you his regards." She had shrugged her shoulders as she had pulled on her gloves. "I thought it best to not say anything to you. But when you asked, I felt guilty about not sharing it."

"I can handle it, Beth." Annabella had lifted a shoulder. "After all, what else can I do?"

Beth had given her a kiss. "As I said earlier...I do not want you to be sad any longer. It is time for some happiness in this family. It is not good for Helen to be surrounded with so many long faces."

She had opened the heavy front door, the cold air swirling into the foyer. "Please tell Helen and Martha about the baby. Daniel is talking with your father today as well. He was seeing to some shipments coming in at the depot." She had waved as she crossed the wide porch, tiny snowflakes swirling about her bundled form.

So, you are married, Orin…and not to me. A sharp, stabbing pain coursed through her chest and tightened around her heart. *Someone else will share your life, bear your children, and make you happy.*

She pulled the heavy quilt over her head and muffled her sobs in the fabric. *I am almost forty years old, Father. No one will ever marry me now. Helen will have no other siblings. I will live here in Rubyville, until everyone dies, and I will be rattling around in this big old house by myself. What is my life worth, Father? Why am I still here?*

"Mama, is it morning yet? I want to play in the snow."

Annabella used the quilt to wipe at her tears, and peered out of her cocoon. Helen's rumpled hair gleamed silver in the moonlight, blue eyes peeking over the edge of the bed. "Is it morning yet?"

"No, my dear, not yet…just a few more hours." Annabella tossed back the covers and slipped from the high bed. She took Helen's hand and guided her to the windows. She leaned down and swung Helen into her arms, placing her upon her hip. She pulled back the lace curtain. "See, it is still dark outside."

Helen shook her head. "Not all the way dark."

Annabella smiled. "That is the moon shining. Is it not pretty? Look how it shines upon the snow…almost silver and blue…rather sparkly."

Helen nodded and leaned her head against her mother. "Pretty."

"It has stopped snowing, but there is plenty to play in when you get up. We can make snow angels and a snowman family. How does that sound?" Annabella kissed the top of Helen's head.

Helen nodded. "I want to sleep with you."

Annabella dropped the curtain. "I think that would be lovely. It will be much warmer than sleeping in our own beds." *Annabella, you should never have Helen sleep with you. She needs to be in her own bed. It teaches her discipline and self-reliance.* Her mother's words came to her in the darkness, nudging at her, making her question her decision.

She walked to the bed and deposited Helen upon it, smiling as the little girl crawled beneath the covers. She climbed in and tucked the covers around them, their heads just peeking out. "Here we are, just as snug as two bugs in a rug."

Helen giggled. "I love you, Mama. You're so silly."

Annabella wrapped her arms around the small form, breathing deeply of her clean, baby-powder scent. "Mama loves you too...*so* much!"

"THANK YOU, MARTHA." ANNABELLA took a sip of the hot tea and closed her eyes. "That just hits the spot." She opened her eyes and set the cup down, wrapping her red fingers around the cup. "I thought I was about frozen. But being outside with Papa and Helen was very enjoyable, I must say."

"Do you not think Helen should have come in? Will she be warm enough?" Martha bustled about the kitchen, shoving another stick of wood into the cook stove. She paused and brushed the back of her wrist against her forehead. "It is warm enough in here, I daresay."

"You need to sit down for a bit and rest. You have been in the kitchen since we went outside, just after breakfast. You work *much* too hard." Annabella shook her head and leaned back in her chair. "And yes, Helen is doing fine. Papa said he would stay down at the barn with her while she helped Peter saddle Misty. It will be nice and warm there."

Martha stopped and placed her reddened hands upon her hips. "Are they going riding in this weather...and with dinner about to be served?"

"No, Papa is going to lead Misty while Helen rides...just around the corral. It will only take a few minutes. Misty is getting rather plump with all the cold weather and Papa thought a bit of exercise would do her good."

"Well, that girl does adore that horse." Martha went to the oven and took out the roasting pan.

"Yes, and she is becoming very good with her balance. It will not be long before she is riding all over the prairie, just as I once did."

Martha chuckled as she uncovered the pot roast and began ladling broth over the meat. "You gave your mother such a scare whenever you were gone like that. She always pictured the worse." She turned to Annabella and shook the ladle at her. "Not to mention riding around in those men's britches. I think that worried her the most."

Annabella laughed. "No one ever saw me. I made sure." She crossed her arms and sighed. "Those were the good old days…so much freedom to do whatever I pleased. I loved riding Strawberry, running like the wind, my hair unbound, and no shoes. There are days now that I would love to do the same."

Martha used the ladle to make her point once again. "Do not be thinking that, my girl. Now that your mother is gone, you are the lady of this house. The good people of Rubyville cannot see you racing through the town in men's britches with your hair a tangled mess, flying behind you. You have a reputation to uphold."

Annabella sighed again. "I know, Martha, but it was a pleasant thought for just a bit."

"You need to be thinking of acting like a grandmother, because that is what you will be come fall." Martha set the roasting pan back in the oven and closed the heavy door. "It is the best news we have heard in this family in a long while."

"I agree. Helen is just beside herself with excitement, even though she does not understand that it will be a long time before she can actually hold the baby." Annabella stood and went to the cupboard. "I think we should eat our dinner in here today. It does not make sense to set that big table in the dining room." She shrugged. "Besides, it is much warmer in here." She reached into the cupboard and took down a stack of plates.

"Suit yourself," shrugged Martha. "I do not think your father will mind and I know I will not miss carrying everything in there. These old bones are more tired than they used to be."

Annabella turned to Martha, holding the plates. "Is there any reason we cannot take our meals in here? Unless we have guests, of course."

"There is no law that says we have to…as far as I know," winked Martha. "Your mother was a stickler for rules, as you remember. She always wanted you, and then Beth and Helen to be taught what was right. She was raised that it was proper that the family took their meals in the dining room, not the kitchen where the help ate their meals."

Annabella set the plates on the long kitchen table. "You have never been considered *the help*, Martha, and you know it." She arranged the plates on the table and went to the drawer for the silverware.

"That is true…but I have had it better than most. Your mama always treated me as family, and that is a fact. For all her uppity ways, she had a gentle heart…and I daresay I miss her greatly." Martha sniffed and took a corner of her large, white apron and dabbed at her eyes.

Annabella went to the older woman and gave her a hug. "I know you do, Martha. You had known her and Aunt Agnes longer than any of us. I know you feel the loss." She kissed the wrinkled cheek. "I am so glad you are here still to care for us and help me with Helen."

Martha pulled away and waved a hand. "Now go on with you. You would do just fine without me and you know it." She bowed her head. "But I am grateful to the Lord above for sending me to your mama when I was only a girl myself. I have had a good life here in the Barton home. That I have." She patted her eyes once more. "Now, enough of this fuss. My dinner will be as black as an old kettle. Where *are* your father and Helen? Dinner will not keep forever."

Chapter Eighteen

October 1907

C HARLES LOOKED UP AT his mother. "I understand, Mama. I will make sure Dottie stays right here where you can see her."

Beth sighed and shook her head as she transferred the eleven-month old Ellen to her other hip. "Well, I hope you understand, Charlie. I just found your sister playing in that big mud puddle in the driveway. I went into the house for just a minute and there she was and you were gone. I have to be able to trust you. Dottie is only three and you are five. You can care for her for just a bit until Helen is home from school. I need to speak with your grandmother."

Charles scratched his blond head and scuffed his shoe on the brown grass. "How long before Helen is home?"

Beth looked at the time-piece hanging on her chatelaine. "She will be here in less than an hour…no time at all. Now run along and play, like a good little boy."

"Yes, Mama." Charles dragged the words out slowly as he turned from the bottom step of the porch.

He took Dottie by the hand. "Come on, we have to play in the grass where it's not muddy. Mama said so."

Beth smiled after her oldest two children and turned as Annabella walked out the front door, closing it behind her. "If you do not mind, I think we had better sit on the porch. Charlie does not want to care for his sister today. I think the barn is calling, and all the joys of being with Peter. Charlie has too many women in his life, I am afraid."

"I do not mind at all. The weather is holding very well for this time of year, and it would be rather pleasant to sit outside for a bit." Annabella gestured to the wicker furniture. "Peter is very popular with Helen as well. Since he and his wife have no children of their own, I think Peter really benefits from Helen and Charlie helping him in the barn. In turn, they benefit from all they have learned about horses and riding."

Beth sat down, her black and white checkered skirt sweeping the porch. She adjusted Ellen on her lap. "Maybe I should send Charlie over now and then. He could help clean the barn, feed the horses. He has so much energy and Daniel just does not have the time to be with him as he would like."

"Is business going well at the hotel?" Annabella took Ellen's chubby hand in hers and shook it up and down, causing the baby to laugh.

"Oh...*very* well." Beth pulled Ellen's dress over her little legs. "I pray it slows down a bit before the holidays. Usually the colder weather stops the traveling for a few months. I am so exhausted that I do not know what to do."

Annabella glanced at Beth's tummy. "Are you expecting again? You know you always feel that way in the beginning."

Beth laughed and shook her head. "No, Mama Bella, I am not expecting. I am very content with the three children we have right now. We have been very blessed...very quickly, I might add." She smiled at Annabella and raised a brow.

Annabella laughed. "I would certainly agree with that." She sat back in her chair, draping her arms over the wicker. "Maybe you should think of having a girl to come in once a day, or even just once a week, to help with the heavier cleaning and laundry. Aunt Agnes and I love to sit with the children whenever you need us to, but that is about all we are able to accomplish." Annabella laughed. "And when we arrive home we have to help one another up the stairs to our rooms."

Beth pursed her lips. "I will think about that. There *are* a couple girls in town that I could ask. Daniel has been after me for a year now to find someone, but I wanted to handle it myself."

"If you are short of funds to pay for someone..." Annabella let her voice trail off.

Beth waved her away. "We are doing very well. The hotel provides for our needs and Mr. Langworthy sends funds every now and then to help with house repairs. We have kept that in the bank in case of some emergency." She adjusted the bonnet over Ellen's light brown curls. "The Lord has taken very good care of us over the years."

Annabella smoothed her charcoal-gray skirt. "How is Mr. Langworthy?"

"He wrote just last week. They have been living in the Pennsylvania area for a few years now. They have two children...a girl and a boy. It sounds as though they are very happy and doing well."

"That is good." Annabella smoothed the stray hairs, touched with gray at her temple. "At least he was able to have a family."

"As do you, Mama Bella." Beth patted the slender hand that lay against the wicker.

Annabella gave a small smile. "Do I seem ungrateful? I do not mean to."

Beth shook her head. "No, you seem sad, as you do every time Mr. Langworthy is mentioned."

"Helen is home!" Charles shouted and pointed at the figure of the ten-year old walking up the drive. Dottie clapped her hands and bounced up and down.

"Please stay right there and wait for her to come to you. I do not want you on the muddy driveway." Beth called to her children as she sat forward and watched.

Annabella laughed. "They are staying right there, Beth. What a temptation for two so young."

"I agree, but it does my heart good to see them obey."

Helen ran the last few feet to Charles and Dottie, giggling as they swooped down on her. The threesome walked to the porch and climbed the steps.

Helen dropped her books upon the porch and reached out for Ellen, the baby wrapping her chubby arms about Helen's neck.

"Welcome home, my dear...did you have a good day at school?" Annabella smiled at her daughter.

Helen shrugged. "About the same as every other day." She kissed Ellen on the cheek. "May we go in and see what Martha has for a snack?"

Annabella nodded. "You may. Aunt Agnes and Martha were working on supper, so please do not get in the way. Be sure to use the kitchen door in case you have mud on your boots. You know how Martha feels about that."

Helen rolled her eyes. "Yes, I know, Mama. We will take our shoes off at the door just in case." She gestured at her school books. "Charlie, could you bring those in for me?"

Charles puffed out his chest. "Of course I can. I am strong." He knelt down and picked up the pile, struggling to his feet. He stumbled along behind his sister and Helen, trying to see over the top of the pile.

Beth gave a big sigh and slumped back in her chair. "Praise God for Helen! The children love her. She is such a big help when she comes over." Beth looked over at Annabella. "Which is what I came to talk with you about."

Annabella frowned. "About Helen helping with the children?"

Beth shook her head. "No, about a problem that Helen is experiencing at school."

"She has not said anything to me about a problem at school. I do not think she enjoys it very much, but I did not either." Annabella crossed her hands before her waist.

Beth rubbed her finger along the edge of the chair arm. "Helen stopped by the house about a week ago, on her way home from school. It seems there are a group of children...three or four...that are making fun of her not having a *real* mother, as they put it."

Annabella sat up straight in her chair. "Not having a *real* mother? Why, of course she does!"

"These children told her that she is just an orphan that you took in...and that is why she does not have a father and why you are not married."

"But that is not true! Helen *is* my daughter! You know that!" Annabella's chest heaved and she gripped the arms of the chair. "I will never understand why children have to be so mean to one another, and lie on top of it."

"They speak the truth, Mama Bella. Maybe in a very hurtful way, but it *is* the truth." Beth spoke softly and slowly.

Annabella stood, her skirt trailing behind as she walked to the porch railing. She gripped the tall white column. "So, it is happening...just as I feared." She leaned her head against the column. "What did you say to her?"

"I told her that you were her mother...that I remembered the day she was born, and that you loved her very much. What *else* was I supposed to say?"

Annabella closed her eyes. "It seems as though you make a mistake in life and it just keeps going around and around to trip you up, and make your life miserable. I wonder why God allows that."

Beth walked to Annabella and laid her head against her shoulder. "Does God allow it…or are we not learning the lessons He has for us?" She kissed Annabella on the cheek and walked around the porch to the kitchen.

ANNABELLA KNOCKED ON HELEN'S bedroom door as she pushed it open. She peered around the dark wood. "May I come in and talk with you a bit before you turn the lights out?"

Helen sat up and set the book she had been reading on the table beside her bed. "Of course, Mama…you always come to tuck me in at night." She lay back down, pulling her covers over her tummy.

Annabella smiled at her daughter. "Yes, I do, but tonight I have to speak with you about something very important. Now that you are ten years old, I think it is time."

She sat on the edge of the bed and faced her daughter. She took her small hand in her own. "You know that you are very, very special to me."

Helen nodded, her blue eyes wide and unblinking.

"Children can be very mean and spiteful at times. They say things to hurt one another. I do not understand why. I assume it is because they feel badly about themselves and they want to belittle someone else, thinking they will feel better. But life does not work that way."

Annabella rubbed her thumb against the back of Helen's hand. "God's Word says we are not to treat others that way…and that when they do treat us badly, we are to ignore it and do what is right for them."

"Pray for them, Mama. Pray that they don't have such a bad attitude anymore…that is what Beth told me."

Annabella smiled. "That is correct. You can pray for those children at school that are treating you badly. Do not say mean things back and try not to take what they are saying as truth."

Helen took her long, blonde braid and started twisting it with one finger. "What if what they are saying *is* true?"

"What are they saying, my dear?" Annabella released Helen's hand and smoothed the back of her hand across Helen's cheek.

Helen looked down at her quilt-covered toes. "They keep saying I am an orphan, and that I don't have real parents. That is why my last name is the same as your last name and why I don't have a father."

She twirled the braid faster. "At first I told them my father had died, but then I don't understand why my last name is the same as yours. Everyone else has their father's last name. Beth was an orphan too and she lived with us, but her last name was Gains, not Barton. Now she is married and her last name is Johnson. Charlie, Dottie and Ellen all have the same last name...Johnson. I don't understand, Mama."

Annabella straightened her shoulders and took a deep breath. "Your father did die, Helen. His name was Thomas Pratt and he was a wonderful man. He spent his life serving God and he is with Him now."

Annabella smiled as she reached out and smoothed her finger along Helen's braid. "You look very much like him. You have the same blue eyes and blonde hair."

"Was he tall? I want to be tall someday." Helen smiled and clasped her hands across her tummy.

"Yes, he was tall. He lived in St. Louis and we met at a church there. It was the same church we volunteered out of...Aunt Agnes, Mr. Pratt, and I. Beth helped as well."

"What did you do when you volunteered?"

"We took meals to people that were sick or not able to leave their homes because they were elderly. Sometimes a family would need help with a new baby. Many people did not have nice homes like ours or money to purchase food and clothing. We also helped at the children's home."

Helen played with her fingers, making a steeple and lacing them together. "Who lived at the children's home?"

"Well, Beth lived at the children's home for a short period of time until Aunt Agnes brought her home to live with us. Her parents had abandoned her."

Helen glanced at her mother. "What does aband...abandon—?"

"Abandoned means that someone is left alone and not cared for. Beth's parents left her, so she did not have anyone to care for her or love her."

Helen nodded her head. "It was good that Aunt Agnes and you took her home with you." She watched her fingers. "So I wasn't left alone?"

Annabella shook her head. "No, you were not left alone. You have lived here in Rubyville since the day you were born, right here in this very house."

"Did my papa love me?" Helen looked at her mother, her blue eyes wide.

"Your papa died before you were born, but he would have loved you very much. He was very good with the children at the home. He enjoyed being with them and reading them stories." Annabella looked away. "He would have loved spending time with you."

"Why is my last name different than my papa's last name? You said his name was Thomas, Thomas—"

"Pratt, Thomas Pratt," Annabella supplied. "I will explain that when you are older and able to understand it better."

"So, I am not an orphan like they say I am?" Helen looked at her mother.

Annabella smiled and shook her head. "No, you are not an orphan. Your father is not here, but you have me, Aunt Agnes, and your grandfather all living right here with you."

"And Martha!" chirped Helen.

"Yes…Martha as well. You have many people that love and care for you." Annabella placed her hand over Helen's hands. "People will always say hurtful things. We cannot stop them or make them change…it is just the way it is. Just remember to not be like that. God says we are to love others as ourselves, and we are to love because He first loved us."

"And if you love someone, you don't say mean things to them." Helen pursed her lips and wrinkled her brow.

Annabella laughed. "If those children could see you now, I do not think they would want to be mean. You look pretty serious." Annabella leaned over, bracing herself with an arm on each side of Helen. She looked into the blue eyes. "I love you so very much, Helen. You are the dearest person in my life. God gave you to me to care for and I will always be here for you."

"I love you too, Mama." Helen wrapped her arms around her mother's neck and hugged her close. "I love my papa too, even though I can't see him and he doesn't know I'm here."

Annabella smiled. "I think he knows."

November 1907

THE HARSH WIND BLEW in cold gusts, sending the shriveled autumn leaves in swirling dances across the sidewalk. Annabella held her feathered hat with one gloved hand as she rushed across the street to the two-storied Barton Mercantile. She opened the door, and hurried into the warm room amidst the jingling of the bell above the door. She closed the door and smoothed the skirt of her plaid walking suit.

"What are you doing out on such a day as this?" William came from behind the counter, brushing his hands on the white apron he wore. "It is much too cold for a walk."

Annabella smoothed her hair. "The cold was not as much of a problem as the wind. I fairly blew here." She opened her small velvet handbag and pulled out a piece of paper.

"Agnes and Martha must have a list of items *absolutely necessary* for the Thanksgiving meal tomorrow." William winked at his daughter as he took the list. His eyes scanned it. "Yes, we have all of this in stock. Just give me a few minutes to get everything together. Then I will drive you home. No need to be walking and carrying purchases across town when I have a perfectly—"

Annabella paused in her perusing of the brightly-patterned material, and gaped at her father. "Papa, you are not suggesting that I go home with you in that, that—"

"It is called an automobile, a Ford model "K" touring automobile, to be precise." He set the cans on the wood counter and reached for a sack of flour. "And yes, I am taking you home in it. We can collect Helen from school as well. You and Martha are the only two that have refused to try it since it arrived last spring."

Annabella repositioned the handbag on her forearm. "I understand that Helen loves to ride in it, and that is just fine. But I prefer to walk."

William shook his head. "Bella, there are times when you can be the most stubborn person I know. But you used to see sense when it was staring at you. Automobiles are the future, and they are here to stay."

"Papa, you are the only person in Rubyville that owns an automobile.

If they are so wonderful, why are the streets not full of them?" Annabella raised one red brow and met her father eye for eye.

"In the bigger cities like Chicago and New York City, the streets *are* full of them. Mark my words, Bella," he shook one, long finger at her, "they are here to stay…and your first ride will be today."

Annabella rolled her eyes. "Well, you might as well set those cans right back on the shelf. There will be three less people around our Thanksgiving table tomorrow. That machine will probably blow up or, or…*something*." Annabella crossed her arms and stared at her father. "It is perfectly fine for you to have a hobby, but I should not have to like it as well."

William chuckled. "You will see. You will be driving in no time."

Chapter Nineteen

THE BARE BRANCHES OF the trees raced by, a gray blur along the road. Annabella held her hat with both hands, the feathers lying flat against the crown. "Is this as fast as we can go?" she called over the roar of the engine. She glanced in the back seat where a smiling Helen sat, gripping the back of the front seat.

"This is as fast as I dare to go. The road is full of holes and difficult to maneuver over. We do not want to get stranded out here with the sun going down soon." William shouted as he turned to Annabella, "You love it!" He laughed. "I knew you would." He turned back to his driving, his black leather gloves gripping the steering wheel. His red hair, white at the temples and streaked silver here and there, stood crazily on his head, his trilby long since given to Helen to hold.

Annabella laughed, her cheeks red from the cold wind, her green eyes dancing. "I do, Papa! This is the most fun I have had in ages." She put one arm up in the air. "I feel like I am flying, and it is *wonderful.*"

"If Grandpapa went faster, we *could* fly," Helen giggled.

William slowed and turned onto the road back into Rubyville. "So, do you want to learn to drive this automobile?"

Annabella smiled. "Do you even have to ask? Is it difficult?"

"Not really. You just need a bit of practice. We can go out on the weekend and I will show you." William drove past the Rubyville Hotel and honked the horn.

"Why did you do that, Grandpapa?" Helen waved to a group of children standing on the porch of the hotel.

"I always honk as I go by. Daniel knows I am out and about, then."

They passed the park on the right and then the church to their left before turning onto the road leading to the Barton home.

William veered off to the right, slowing as he drove down the driveway. He stopped beside the back porch. "You girls can get out here. I will park this and be in soon. I may speak with Peter first."

He slid out of the front seat and opened the back door for Helen, taking his trilby from her and placing it upon his head.

Helen jumped from the vehicle. "Thank you, Grandpapa. That was so much fun!" Her blue eyes danced as she looked up at her grandfather.

William took the box of packages from the floor and carried them to the porch. "You are welcome, my dear. I had fun as well." He gave Helen a wink. "I think your mother rather enjoyed it."

Annabella walked around the front of the touring automobile, her eyes taking in every feature. "I did, and I cannot wait until the weekend." She ran her gloved hand along the back of the tufted leather seat. "It really is rather magnificent."

William smiled at his daughter. "I could not agree with you more. I think it is the best purchase I ever made."

He slid back into the front seat and gripped the wheel. "I am going to put her away for the night." He tipped his hat as he proceeded toward the barn.

Annabella and Helen climbed the steps to the porch.

"Why did Grandpapa call the automobile a *her*?" Helen looked at her mother as they walked to the kitchen door.

"I do not know, my dear." Annabella gave her handbag to Helen as she picked up the box. "That is a question for your grandfather to answer."

They stood by the kitchen door as they watched William park the automobile beneath the roof on the west side of the barn that had been built the previous summer.

"Grandpapa won't be in for a long time, will he?" Helen shook her head, watching as William covered the automobile with a huge piece of canvas. Peter came out of the barn and took one side, helping to straighten it.

"No, Helen, he will not." Annabella opened the kitchen door, balancing the box. "We will tell Martha that Papa is down at the barn. I am sure she will want to start supper without him...again."

ANNABELLA ENTERED THE PARLOR and took a seat on the end of the sofa. She turned to her aunt, seated at the opposite end, reading a book. "Martha went to bed and Helen is all settled for the night as well." She heaved a sigh and clasped her hands in her lap.

"I am sure Helen is tired out after that ride this afternoon." Agnes turned to her brother-in-law. "She could not stop talking about it all through supper."

William turned a page of the paper and snapped it open. He sat with one knee over the other, his elbows upon the chair arms. "Yes, that child can chatter when she gets a mind to." He lowered his paper and looked at Annabella. "I remember someone else doing the same. It drove Lavinia to distraction."

He laid the paper across his lap and turned to the fire crackling beside his chair. "She has been gone six years…difficult to imagine."

Agnes nodded and closed the book. "I think that is why Martha retires so early now. She and Lavinia used to visit in the evenings while they did their needlework. It was their time to catch up on the events of the day."

Annabella smiled. "You mean the gossip of Rubyville."

Agnes returned the smile. "Yes, that too." She looked at William. "Lavinia and Martha were together most of their lives. I am sure Martha misses her greatly."

William cleared his throat and nodded before taking up the paper.

Agnes set the book upon the sofa and adjusted her position to face Annabella. "So when do the driving lessons commence?"

"Papa said this weekend." Annabella smiled, her eyes dancing. "I am really excited. Who knew it would be so much fun to ride in an automobile? I cannot imagine why they were not invented ages ago."

"Everything has its time, my dear." William spoke from behind the paper. "The horse has been around for centuries as a mode of transportation. It has sufficed, and it will for people for many years to come."

Agnes turned her head to speak to the back of the paper. "Since you are willing to teach Annabella to drive, I would like to learn as well, William. In St. Louis you cannot cross a street without one almost running you down. I have been fascinated by them since I first saw them. I think this Mr. Henry Ford is going to do very well for himself."

"I agree with you there, Agnes. From everything I have been reading about the man, he will have an automobile in every household before long." William turned another page of the paper.

Annabella shook her head. "Can you imagine?"

Agnes nodded. "Actually I can. If the price goes down a bit, I may consider purchasing one for myself."

William crumpled the paper on his lap. "*You* would purchase an automobile? Whatever would you do with it?" He harrumphed before snapping out the paper.

"The same thing you do with yours, William. What a silly question." Agnes smiled and gave Annabella a wink. "Men are not the only people that may travel." Agnes smoothed the skirt of her brown dress. "I may even take a trip with it."

"That is preposterous!" William crumpled the paper once again. "It would be very dangerous for you to be driving around by yourself. You already take that bicycle of yours all over Rubyville." William's green eyes darkened as he stared at his sister-in-law.

"Yes, I do and I will continue to do so. It is a very pleasant activity. I enjoy it much more than I ever did riding a horse." Agnes patted her brown hair. "They can be terrible beasts when they set their minds to it."

"You will never forget that horse running away with you, will you?" William shook his head. "It was not the horse's fault."

Annabella sat forward and glanced at her father and then Agnes. "I do not think I have heard this one before. I did not realize you harbored a dislike of horses." She frowned. "Although, now that I think about it, you never would go riding with me."

"That is a fact. They are huge beasts with a mind of their own. I prefer to stay away when possible." Agnes's fingers fussed with the lace at her neck. "Helen spends much of her time down in the barn with Misty. I pray Peter is teaching her to be careful of the great beast."

William scoffed. "Misty is Helen's most adored companion. Peter has taught her everything he knows about horses…how to care for them and how to ride. She will be a great horsewoman someday."

Annabella held up a hand. "I want to hear the reason behind your dislike of horses, Aunt Agnes."

"It is not important now…and too many years have passed to recall." Agnes picked up her book and made a good show of reading.

William folded the paper and laid it on the table beside the chair. "It was shortly after your mother and I were married, so Agnes must have been about twelve—"

Agnes lowered the book. "I was thirteen years old."

William rolled his eyes. "Your aunt was thirteen years old. The three of us had gone for a picnic, not far from where the soddy stood. Storm clouds began to gather in the west, so we decided to head home. Each of us mounted our horses and just as we started back, there was a loud crack of thunder—"

"It came from nowhere." Agnes's brown eyes were wide, as if she was experiencing the storm once more.

William looked at Agnes. "You seem to recall the details just as well as I…why do you not finish the story?"

Agnes lifted the book. "You are doing just fine, William, please continue."

William shook his head. "The thunder did a fair job of spooking all our horses, but Agnes had a young mare and she bolted."

"Everyone says a horse will go back to the barn, but not this one." Agnes closed the book and laid it on her lap. "That horse ran for her life and I hung on for mine. By the time your father was able to ride up next to me and get her calmed down, the storm was upon us. There was lightning flashing everywhere, rain coming down in buckets."

"One of those Kansas summer storms that come upon you…gone just as quickly as they rumble in." William uncrossed his legs and stood.

He knelt in front of the fire and moved the logs with the poker. "Your mother had the good sense to go into the trees beside the river where there was some protection."

Agnes put one hand to her chest. "I was, and never have been, so frightened in my life. Not even when the tornado went through St. Louis."

Annabella took her aunt's hand. "But as Papa said, it was not the horse's fault…just an unforeseen set of circumstances. At least no one was hurt."

William stood and set the poker in the stand. "No, we all survived it. I eventually sold that mare, though. She was always skittish after that and whenever a storm came rolling in, she just about went crazy."

Annabella shook her head. "Poor thing...it was not her fault."

William checked his pocket watch and stuffed it back in the intended spot. "It is past my bed time."

He patted his lean abdomen. "I want to make sure that I am well-rested tomorrow. Better to enjoy that delicious Thanksgiving meal that Martha and Agnes have prepared."

Annabella and Agnes gave the expected laugh as he walked from the room and headed up the stairs.

Agnes leaned against the back of the sofa, and draped one arm along the scrolled rosewood. "I have been meaning to talk with you about Helen. Beth said she spoke with you a few weeks ago about the teasing at school."

"I think *teasing* is too kind of a word for it. I may go and speak with the parents about what has been going on." Annabella crossed her arms and drummed her fingers against the sleeves of her blouse. "Children can be so mean to one another. If anyone is different, it seems to be an opportunity to call names, ignore or just make life miserable for that person." She shook her head. "I will never understand it."

"It has been going on since time began and I daresay it will continue. It is in the sin nature to strike out and hurt...especially if one is jealous or envious of another." Agnes reached out and laid her hand on Annabella's shoulder. "You do understand that it would be a bad idea to speak with the parents of the children?"

Annabella frowned. "No, I see no reason why I should cower and let them treat Helen in such a way."

Agnes clasped her hands in her lap. "Children rarely speak of things...such as what is being said to Helen...all on their own. They usually have heard them somewhere else...by someone they respect or look up to."

Annabella slid her hands to her lap and gaped at Agnes. "Are you trying to tell me that these children heard these lies from their parents?"

Agnes nodded. "That is what I fear."

"Have you heard gossip around town about this?"

"I have not, but Beth mentioned that Daniel has heard talk, and I know your father has as well."

Annabella slapped her hands against her legs. "Why have I not been told? This has probably gone on for years. I have not heard anything."

Agnes's brow wrinkled. "People are going to be careful and not say things around you, Annabella. The Barton name is something to be respected in Rubyville."

"Then why has Papa heard talk?"

"Your father is out and about every day…working at the store, the depot, and visiting Daniel at the hotel. He has overheard snippets of conversations over the years." Agnes rubbed her brow. "Annabella, you knew this was going to be a problem. Talking to the parents with the attitude you have will only make the situation worse."

Annabella stood and crossed her arms, staring down at her aunt. "Yes, I knew it was going to be a problem…which is why I did not like Mama's plan to just let people think Helen was an orphan I had adopted. I did not want to lie about Helen's birth." Annabella threw down her arms and clenched her hands into fists. "But I never thought people would take my indiscretions out on my child."

"Children are an easy target. They are young and naïve."

Annabella turned with a swirl of her plaid skirt. She walked to the turreted windows. "To think the people of Rubyville are attacking my daughter in this way makes me livid."

She turned to her aunt. "Why, if Papa had not started this town and put so much money into it, it would not even be here. Why would the *good people* of Rubyville attack our family in this way?" Annabella stared at her aunt, green eyes flashing.

"Just because William Barton founded Rubyville, does not make you or your family immune to real life. People will be people, with all their warts and insufficiencies exposed at one time or another. That is why we all need Christ as our Savior and His Father in our lives, guiding us and directing our paths. The Bible shows us the way and evens out all those inconsistencies we all have."

Annabella set her hands on her hips, eyes flashing. "Well…what am I supposed to do? You said speaking to the parents with my bad attitude would not be a good idea."

"I think it would stir up more gossip and make Helen's life at school more miserable than it already is." Agnes shook her head. "For you to reprimand the parents and ask them to control their children's tongues while at school will only make the parents angry." Agnes looked at her niece. "Annabella, the entire town knows that Helen was conceived out of wedlock. They know you have lied to them all these years, or at least tried to cover up what you did. It makes you seem common in their eyes."

Annabella rubbed her temples. "None of this is any of their business. Why do I owe anyone an explanation? Why can they not train their children to be loving and kind?"

"How they train their children is between them and the Lord, they are not accountable to you. Annabella, please look at me," requested Agnes. When the green eyes met hers, she continued. "Annabella, you have said you are a Believer. You have a testimony to live here in this town. Having a child out of marriage is frowned upon and goes against what God has taught us in the Bible. But it does happen. It happened to you." Agnes stood and walked over to Annabella. "I never agreed with Lavinia's plan. I felt it was hiding from the truth. But your mother is no longer here. If you feel the need to talk with the parents, do it out of a spirit of love for them, their children and your daughter. Admit that what you did was wrong, but you have a daughter and you do not want to see her hurt. It probably will not stop the gossip, and it may become worse for awhile."

"How is that good or any better?" Annabella looked up, blinking back the tears.

"It is better and right because you are honest and not running away from the truth. Live your life here in Rubyville as a testimony to what God has done for you and Helen…how He has provided. You will gain people's respect, I guarantee it."

"So what do I do? Stand in the middle of the park and announce that I am a fallen woman with a child…they can throw stones if they like?" Annabella brushed the tears from her cheeks.

Agnes smiled. "I daresay that any of them are without sin in their own lives and that they could throw the first stone." She took Annabella's hand. "Just live your life, honoring God and what He has done for you. Address the whispered comments as they come up, with love and patience. Helen told me about your conversation the other night. I think you have given her the information she needs to know for now. She is so happy to know she has a *real* father." She patted Annabella's hand. "In time, you will have to give her more information, when she is older and understands."

Annabella reached out and wrapped her arms around her aunt. "Will I ever have the correct answers and handle situations as I should?"

Agnes smoothed her hand over Annabella's back. "You will, dear. It just takes a lot of living for some people."

Annabella laughed, "I do not think that is a complimentary statement. There are not enough years left in my life to reach that goal, I am afraid."

Chapter Twenty

July 1912

D R. RUNDELL LABORED DOWN the stairs, one gnarled hand gripping the railing. He paused at the foot of the staircase and reached into his pocket, pulling out a white handkerchief. He mopped his brow and returned the linen to its rightful place. He looked at Annabella, standing in the arched doorway leading into the parlor, and held out his hand. "Please help an old man to a chair, my dear."

"Of course, may I get you something to drink? Martha just made a fresh pitcher of lemonade." Annabella took the frail hand and placed her hand beneath his elbow, walking with him to the parlor.

"Martha's lemonade would just hit the spot. I am in need of a little refreshment." He nodded to the women gathered in the parlor and then gestured to the blonde-haired fifteen year-old. "Helen, would you please get my bag from your grandfather's room?" He scratched his white head as he sat down. "I must have left it, but I do not think I would have made it down the stairs with it anyway." He leaned back in the chair and sighed. "This is why I retired all those years ago. Just cannot do the job anymore."

Martha returned with a tall glass of lemonade and handed it to the older man. "There is plenty more if you are in need of it."

"Thank you, Martha." Dr. Rundell lifted the glass to the white-haired woman and then drank the contents. He finished the last of it with a sigh and brushed at his white beard. "I may just survive the rest of this day to see my first great-grandchild."

"I do apologize for calling you out, Dr. Rundell…and on such a hot day. But when Papa arrived home for supper, he just did not seem like himself. With your son out on a call and your grandson delivering his

163

first baby…your great-grandchild no less, I did not know what else to do." Annabella wrapped her arms about her waist.

Dr. Rundell waved a hand at her. "It was no problem. I have been checking in on your family for almost twenty years. It has just been a busy day in the doctoring business. It just happens that way at times." He chuckled. "You would think with three Rundell doctors in this little town, we would be well covered."

Helen entered the room and carried the black bag to the doctor.

"Just set it right down, my dear. I need to speak with all of you and get a bit of a rest before I leave." He looked at Helen. "Was your grandfather lying down as I instructed him to do?"

Helen nodded. "He was sleeping." She brushed her long, straight hair from her shoulder and took a seat next to Beth on the sofa. The older woman took Helen's hand and gave her a smile before setting her gaze on the doctor.

Agnes looked at Annabella and then addressed Dr. Rundell. "Is there anything we need to be concerned with? Is William alright?"

Dr. Rundell scratched his white beard. "To put it simply, William is worn out. His heart is weak. Working like he did today, down at the depot, in this heat…" He shook his head. "Well, it sure did not help him any."

Annabella set her hands upon her hips. "He told me he was just visiting with Mr. Norton." She sighed and shook her head. "What am I going to do with him?"

Dr. Rundell chuckled. "William Barton is not going to slow down, my dear. It is not in his nature. He has had a good life and he is ready to go home and join his wife."

"He said that?" Beth gaped at the doctor. "I did not think he was ready to…ready to—"

"Die?" Dr. Rundell gave a half-smile. "You are young yet, my dear. There will come a time when you have lived your life to the fullest and you are ready to meet your Creator." He sighed. "I am ready as well. The Lord knows that. If you remember, I have a few years on William."

"But you have a new grandbaby coming." Helen looked at the doctor, her blue eyes wide. "Don't you want to be here to watch him or her grow?"

Dr. Rundell nodded. "It is a might tempting, but that baby will grow with or without me being here. I have welcomed so many babies into this world…and it has been a pleasure. It is the best part of doctoring." He gestured to Beth. "Your three oldest if I remember correctly. That youngest one…" he frowned at Beth.

"Georgie," she supplied with a smile.

He snapped his fingers. "That is the one. That little man was in a big hurry, and he still is."

Beth laughed and nodded her head. "That he is."

"Anyway," he struggled to stand, his arms shaking with the effort of pushing up from the chair. "I had best be going."

Annabella rushed to his side and took his arm. "Helen will get your hat and cane." She walked with him to the front door, Agnes, Martha, and Beth trailing behind. "Is there anything we can do for Papa to help him be more comfortable? Make him stay home, lie down—"

Dr. Rundell stopped and shook one bent finger at Annabella. "You *encourage* him to do what he is physically able to do and what makes him happy. William knows what he wants."

Agnes laid a hand on the old man's arm. "How much time does William have? Maybe a year or so—"

"A few weeks, maybe months…not much more." Dr. Rundell set his bowler hat on his white head. "I pray he goes in his sleep, having a dream about that automobile he loves to drive around the countryside. What a way to walk into Heaven and greet all those that have gone before." He took his cane from Helen. "If you could please get my bag from the parlor and set it on the seat of the carriage I would be much obliged."

"Of course," answered Helen as she hurried to the parlor.

"You ladies have a good evening." Dr. Rundell tipped his hat and took the arm Helen offered as they exited the house.

Annabella wrapped her arms about her waist and turned to the three women standing in the foyer. "I guess that is the end of it." Her gaze traveled up the stairs. "I am going to check on Papa and see if there is anything he needs."

November 1912

ANNABELLA STOOD IN THE early November sunshine, the cold wind lifting the black veil of her hat. Her green eyes followed the large crowd walking from the small cemetery behind the church. Their bowed heads and black clothing seeming to darken the sunny skies. Helen walked with Beth, one arm wrapped about Beth's waist. Martha and Agnes leaned on one another, Martha's shoulders shaking, a white handkerchief held to her nose.

Annabella looked away and set her gaze upon the headstone beside the huge pile of dirt. *Lavinia Saunders Barton, born in 1846, died in 1901, beloved wife and mother. You are with her now, Papa...and all those babies you never had a chance to name and watch grow. I know you are happy...and I am happy for you too...really. I just miss you so much!* She sank to the cold, brown grass, her black dress pooling around her. *Rubyville will not be the same without you, Papa. This town is yours...your creation and your dream. How will it succeed without you?* She covered her face with her black-gloved hands and rocked back and forth, sobs shaking her body.

"You will make yourself sick, Annabella...sitting on the cold, wet ground." Strong arms pulled her up.

Annabella stared at the gray-haired man before her, the well-remembered dark eyes searching her face, the gray mustache flecked with white. "Orin?" Annabella pressed her cheek to his shoulder and placed her hands at his back. "How did you know I would need you so?"

Orin held her, one hand smoothing her back. He closed his eyes for a moment and breathed deeply. "I never meant to intrude. Beth called me and told me your father had passed away. I took the first train I could to be here in time for the funeral...to pay my respects. He was a great man. I was proud to have known him and worked with him all those years ago. But I did not want to bother you. My intention was to leave immediately...but I could not when I saw you here."

Annabella sniffed, her words muffled against his shoulder. "I cannot go on, Orin. I have lost everything. There is no purpose in being here. Rubyville will fall into ruin with my father gone, people will move away." She sniffed again. "There will be no one left here that cares."

Strong hands gripped her shoulders and pushed her away. He bent his head and captured her eyes with his. "I do not want to hear that kind of talk. Rubyville means everything to you. It is your legacy to pass down to your daughter. You have been a part of this town since the day you were born and you will be, until the day you die. Your father is gone, but you understand his dreams, and Rubyville will continue on and grow."

Annabella lowered her eyes. "I wish that were all true." She looked up, her eyes searching his through the netting of the veil. "This would have all been so much easier with you here, beside me. I am so tired of struggling and being alone."

Orin let his hands fall to his sides. "Our lives did not work out that way, Annabella. I have a wonderful wife and two children that mean the world to me." He looked over at the church and then turned back to her. "You have a family here...your daughter, your aunt, Beth and Daniel with their four children. You have been blessed in so many ways. You are not alone."

"But I do not have a husband to share my life with. I missed both opportunities for marriage, Orin...all because of my irrational and immature behavior." She held up her skirt and stepped through the grass. "I will pay the price for that the rest of my life."

"You really should not see it in that manner. You have had opportunities that many women never experience. You are independent and strong-willed, not a good combination for a married woman. Many men could not and would not handle that."

She stopped and looked at him. "You would have."

He gave her a smile. "Yes, I would have, but it would have been an exhausting proposition."

She shook her head and continued her progress from the cemetery. "I see you still remember how to fit in a little jab now and then."

"Annabella, I must say, the verbal exchanges with you over the years have been missed. You stir something in me that lights a spark, and makes me feel alive." He gave her a wide smile, his white teeth standing out against the gray of his mustache.

"Well, better a spark than a flame, I suppose. We would have been consumed." She shook out her skirt as she stepped to the sidewalk in front of the church.

Orin threw back his head and laughed. "That is true."

Annabella put a finger to her pursed lips, her gaze sweeping the town. "You should not be laughing. Not today. What will people think?"

Orin shook his head. "Annabella, your father loved life and saw the best side of anything and everything. He is so happy right now, that I do not think he would begrudge us a little laughter down here." He looked up at the blue sky. "Why, he is probably doing a jig with your mother this very minute." He eyes lowered, twinkling merrily. "Your mother is not worried about the rules of society any longer and she is dancing right along with him."

Annabella smiled, her green eyes brimming over once more. "I think you are probably right. I miss them so much!"

"And you always will, my dear. But the sharpness of the pain will lessen." He watched as she brushed at her cheek with a dainty handkerchief. "Now…no more crying. I will walk you home so that you have time to fill me in on everything that has happened in Rubyville over the past ten years."

Annabella dabbed at her eyes. "I know for a fact that Beth has kept you informed very well over the years."

Orin nodded. "Yes, she has. But I want to hear it from you. Her letters have been more about Daniel and the children, which I have loved reading about." He held out his arm. "But I want to hear all about Helen. She has grown into a beautiful woman."

Annabella wrapped her hand around the offered arm. "Yes, she has. She is fifteen, almost sixteen, in January. I cannot imagine where the years have flown. She is so very much like Thomas. She is slow to speak and make decisions…very thoughtful…everything that I am not."

"Does she have friends, a young man that is special?" They stopped at the edge of the street for a passing wagon.

"I was very sorry to hear of your loss, ma'am." The farmer from the wagon called out. "Mr. Barton was a man to look up to, that he was. He

168

will be missed around here." He tipped his hat and continued on.

Annabella lifted a hand and called out, "Thank you for your kind words."

They crossed the street and Annabella continued the conversation. "Helen has never made friends easily. She has girls at school that she takes walks with occasionally, and a couple of them have come over for dinner, but no one that she spends a lot of time with. There are no special young men that I am aware of." They veered off the road and continued up the long driveway to the Barton home. "You may want to ask Beth that question. She and Helen spend much time conversing about things Helen would never discuss with me."

"And why is that?"

Annabella lifted a shoulder. "I have never understood why. I have always tried to make myself available to Helen, and show her that I love her." She narrowed her eyes as she looked at the large, white house at the end of the drive. "She has always sought Beth rather than me."

"Well, I am sure Helen sees Beth as a sister...the only one she has known. Since they are closer in age, she probably feels more comfortable talking with her about certain subjects." He patted her hand that lay across his arm. "You have done a wonderful job raising Beth. I would not be too concerned with Helen. She is at an age where she has to figure some things out."

"The raising of Beth and Helen has been a group effort. I would never have been able to do it without my parents, Aunt Agnes, and Martha. They have always been willing and able to step in where I have been lacking."

Orin stopped and took her hands in his. "Now those are some of the blessings that I was speaking of before. You are not alone, Annabella. You have many people that love you and care about your well-being. Let them help you through this difficult time."

Annabella gave him a half-smile. "I do appreciate you coming today. I know Beth will be so happy to see you and introduce you to her little brood."

"From her letters, I do not think her brood is so *little*." He chuckled. "That youngest one, Georgie, seems to keep her pretty busy."

Annabella laughed. "He does. He is always one step ahead of everyone else. He makes a monthly trip to see Dr. Rundell for one reason or another." She shook her head, her cheeks glowing. "If he had been born first, I am afraid he may have been an only child."

Orin gripped her hands tighter. "It is so good to see you smile. Remember those blessings I was telling you about. Your cup is full and running over, Annabella. Thank God for all that you have."

HELEN STOOD AT THE dining room window, her blue eyes narrowing as she watched the couple just beyond the porch. They held hands, her mother smiling at the gray-haired man in a way that she had never seen before.

Martha carried in a large bowl of mashed potatoes, fluffy and white, melting squares of butter peeking here and there. "I think the rolls are ready to come out of the oven, Helen, if you would not mind tending to them. I have set a basket on the kitchen table that you may use. We could have many people coming through here today offering their condolences. I want to make sure there is plenty of food for everyone." Martha stepped back from the table and wiped her hands on her large apron. "Helen, did you hear me, girl?"

"Who is that man in the front yard with Mama? He seems vaguely familiar to me." Helen continued watching the pair.

Martha walked over and peered through the lace curtain as Beth carried in a large platter of sliced beef. She set it on the table and walked to the window as well.

"What are we doing?" Beth asked as she peered between Martha and Helen. She squinted and clapped her hands together. "Why, that is Mr. Langworthy. He was able to come after all. Mama Bella must be thrilled." She untied her apron and laid it across the back of a chair as she swept from the room.

Martha nodded her white head and placed her hands at her ample hips. "That it is. Mr. Langworthy himself."

Helen crossed her arms and fingered the black lace at her throat. She watched as Beth hugged Mr. Langworthy and then gestured toward the house. "Have I met him before?"

"That you did." Martha adjusted the apron at her waist and turned back to the long dining table, laden with food. "You must have been about four or five years old at the time. It was the summer Beth and Daniel were married. I remember, because Mr. Langworthy left just after the wedding ceremony."

"And he has not returned to Rubyville since then?" Helen lifted the curtain aside and peered at the threesome walking toward the wide porch of the house.

Martha shook her head. "Not that I recall. Now you need to tend to those rolls. They will be burnt black and no use to any of us."

"Do you know anything else about Mr. Langworthy?" Helen dropped the curtain and turned to the older woman.

Martha frowned and waved a hand in Helen's direction. "Go on with you now. I know plenty about the man. He was the one your mother was to marry all those years ago, but she ran away." She shook her head. "Those rolls will be blacker than the coals in the fire. I do not have time to fill you in on over twenty-five years of trouble, and you do not have time to listen, my girl." She bustled into the kitchen, her voice a low grumble.

Helen looked over her shoulder and watched as the man helped her mother up the stairs. *You would think she was ninety years old. To be smiling and laughing on the day Grandpapa is buried. Why, Grandmama would have been appalled at such behavior.*

She flipped her straight, blonde hair behind her shoulder and hurried into the kitchen.

Chapter Twenty One

BETH TOOK A DEEP breath of the cold air and linked her arm through Helen's. She nudged the younger woman's shoulder with her own. "I am *so* ready for a nice, long walk. I really appreciated your help with the children today. I was able to get a few chores taken care of that have been needing my attention." They walked across the expansive yard of the Langworthy home, their booted feet crunching on the brown, dry grass.

"You know I love to spend time with you and the children. It helps with the boredom. You can embroider only so many items in a house." Helen smiled at Beth, her blue eyes sparkling. She looked up at the gray sky and sighed. "I do hope we get more snow. I adore snow, and it seems to snow so rarely here."

Beth laughed. "You could move to Vermont or New York. I have read that it snows quite often there."

"You are laughing, but I *have* thought seriously of moving to the east, when I leave school." Helen brushed the stray, blonde hairs from her red cheeks. "I know I want to see much more of the world than Rubyville, Kansas."

They approached the line of trees along the river, the stark branches reaching into the scudding, gray clouds. The water flowed through the rocks in the riverbed, correcting its course when met with frozen, jagged ice. The tall grass beside the trees rustled in the drone of the Kansas wind.

"You can have the rest of the world, my dear. I remember St. Louis when I was a girl and I do not miss a thing about it. There were always too many people, hurrying everywhere, too many buildings blocking out the sunshine." She pulled her arm from Helen's and took her gloved hand. "I am very satisfied to stay in Rubyville the rest of my days."

Helen glanced at Beth. "There must have been things you enjoyed about St. Louis. It could not have been *all* bad."

Beth frowned, wrinkling her brow. "I loved Lafayette Park. Mama Bella and I spent much of our time there. It had a tall, black iron fence around it and so many huge trees. It was like a canopy in the summer." She shook her head. "But the tornado all but destroyed it." She squeezed Helen's hand. "Come, let us talk about more cheerful things. How do you feel being sixteen years old now?"

Helen laughed. "About the same as being fifteen." She shrugged. "Truly, that is what it is like. I still have to finish school, and have the same routine I have had my entire life. Nothing exciting ever happens around here, Beth."

"You have to make life what you want it to be, Helen. You can be just as content here in Rubyville as in St. Louis or Chicago or even New York City. Changing your geographical location does not guarantee happiness."

"I understand that, but I do not agree with that statement." Helen kicked at a large rock in her path. "I cannot accept that there are not more interesting people and places outside of Rubyville." She stopped and pulled her hand from Beth's hand. "If you are in a big city there are so many more opportunities for you. There are schools and theaters, large stores, and people that can converse on many topics, rather than what the weather is for the day." She clenched her hands at her sides and smiled. "It is exciting just thinking of all the possibilities waiting for me!"

Beth looked toward where the Barton home stood in the distance, the dark slate roof protecting the large, white edifice. "Does Mama Bella know you have plans to leave Rubyville as soon as you are able?"

"No, I rarely talk with Mama about anything. She does not care to hear my opinion and it would not make a difference to her whether I was here or not." Helen crossed her arms and stubbed the toe of her boot against the dry ground.

Beth turned to Helen. "How could you say such a thing? Your mother loves you and you mean the world to her. She will be devastated to learn that you want to leave...especially after losing her father just a few months ago."

"She will not be *devastated*, Beth." Helen looked over her shoulder toward the house she had grown up in. "Besides, she has Aunt Agnes and Martha."

"They do not replace her daughter."

Helen looked at Beth. "Please forgive me if I sound bitter, but Mama has always thought of you more as her daughter than I."

Beth shook her head. "That is not true, Helen. Your mother and Aunt Agnes have been wonderful and gracious toward me, all my life. They have treated me as their daughter and I have loved being part of the Barton family." She reached out and took Helen's hand. "But that relationship has never, *ever* replaced you."

Helen pulled away, her blue eyes flashing. "Then why did she deny my existence as her daughter for most of my life? The others at school still talk about me when they think I cannot hear them. They say I was just another sweet child that Mama took in out of the goodness of her heart."

Beth rubbed her brow. "You know that is not true. Mama Bella explained all that to you years ago."

"Not to my satisfaction." Helen spun around and walked into the trees, stopping to lean against the charcoal gray of a trunk. She pulled at the rough bark with one finger.

Beth followed, lifting her wool skirt from the tall weeds and grass of the previous summer. "Helen, you need to talk with Mama Bella about all of this. You are being eaten with a cancer that will only become worse if you do not take care of it."

Helen narrowed her blue eyes at Beth. "I do not want to speak with my mother about anything. She will only lie to me more…and hide…hide behind her Bible rather than give me true answers."

Beth squared her jaw. "I will not listen to you disrespect God's Word. You have been taught to respect your Creator and abide in His Word."

Helen looked at the ground. "I am sorry, Beth. I do respect God and what He has done for us, sending His Son to die for us. But I cannot respect what my own mother has done."

"Then maybe you do not understand what has taken place. Maybe you have your facts jumbled and strewn about, rather than in order as you should have before you accuse someone."

Helen took a deep breath. "Mama is in love with that Mr. Langworthy that was here for Grandpapa's funeral, is she not?"

"You really need to speak with your mother—"

"My *mother* dances around the truth and tries to make it sound correct and decent. The very same thing she has accused her own mother of doing." Helen reached out and touched Beth's shoulder. "I just need to hear the truth…once and for all. It will not be from my mother."

Beth's blue eyes darkened to a slate gray. "Do you *really* want the truth, Helen? Or are you looking for more reasons to build a wall between you and your mother? I have observed you with your mother over the past few years. No matter what she does or says to you, you push her away. You will not allow her to love you. Why, Helen? What has she done to hurt you so badly?"

"She denied me my father. She loved another man…that Mr. Langworthy that was here."

Beth placed her back against the tree trunk, her eyes sweeping across the river and the woods beyond. "Your father died in that tornado, and you know that. Your father *did not* die because your mother loved someone else."

"Can you be sure of that?" Helen caught Beth's gaze. "From what I understand, my father had asked Mama to marry him several times over the years. She kept denying him. If she had married him when he asked, I would have been born *after* they were married and I would not have lived a life of shame because of my mother's sin life. They would have been married and probably living here in Rubyville, far from that tornado."

"And if I had married John D. Rockefeller I would have been a very wealthy woman and of course happy…because that is all that matters." Beth shook her head with a furrowed brow as she shoved her gloved hands into the pockets of her wool coat.

"He would have been about sixty years old when you were old enough to marry…much too old for you." Helen smiled at Beth.

Beth returned the smile, shaking her head. "I do not think you have shared this side of your personality with your mother. She thinks you are quiet and thoughtful, much like your father. She does not realize that you are more like her than she would imagine." She reached out and smoothed Helen's long, blonde hair. "You are very much like your grandfather as well."

"I hope so, Beth. He had such a great attitude about life. I really miss him, you know." Helen bit her lower lip and blinked rapidly.

"I know you do. Just remember that your mother does, as well. She needs you right now, Helen. She needs you to love her as your mother and not hold bitterness for transgressions that happened long ago." Beth pushed away from the tree and continued walking. "Believe me, your mother has suffered greatly for her actions. She knows what she did was wrong. God established orderliness for our lives. He designed marriage and the blessings of children in it." She stopped and turned to Helen. "But God is also gracious and merciful toward us. He is there for us when we fall; He picks us up and gives us another chance...over and over again. He does not love any of us any less because of the sin in our lives or because we make wrong decisions. But there are consequences for our actions. That is why we all should choose wisely."

"But my mother has not been the only one that has paid a price for what she did. I have paid it, Aunt Agnes has...we have all heard gossip, and observed people snickering behind their hands." Helen pulled the velvet collar of her tweed coat higher against her chin. "That does not seem fair to me."

Beth shrugged. "I know it does not, but God is always fair. He knows what He is doing." Beth shivered. "We should head back. That wind is becoming very cold." She took Helen's hand. "Just remember, God knows what happened between your parents. You were the blessing that came out of that union. Do not let people cloud your judgment about the best way to handle that in your own life. People can be very condemning and downright mean. You need to be patient and loving toward them and apply God's Word to your own life. You cannot change others, only yourself."

ANNABELLA PACED THE LENGTH of the parlor, her black-colored serge dress flowing about her ankles. She crossed her arms at her waist and fingered the white lapels of her bodice. "I appreciate you letting me know about your conversation with Helen." Annabella's green eyes glanced from Beth to Agnes, seated together on the parlor sofa. "I have known she is not pleased with me for some time now. I just have not known what to do about it."

Agnes looked down at her clasped hands resting in her lap. "I do not think there is anything you *can* do about it. It seems from what Beth has said that Helen is a very bitter young woman right now. I do not think she wants to hear the truth or any explanation of what really happened. She has her mind made up about what she *thinks* happened."

Beth sighed and smoothed the stray curls back from her center part and patted the low pompadour. "I am afraid Aunt Agnes is correct. She feels this is her 'cross to bear' at this point in her life, and she is rather relishing in it."

Annabella paused and placed her hands on her slim hips. "What nonsense about me being in love with Orin Langworthy! She comes to that conclusion from watching us talking in the front yard?" She shook her head. "And for her to think that is the reason for Thomas dying."

Agnes cleared her throat, glancing at Beth before catching Annabella's eyes and holding them. "She does have a point to be made there, Annabella."

Annabella slid her hands from her hips and stared at her aunt. She turned her back to the two women. "Yes, I loved Orin and…and I probably still do. I never loved Thomas in that way, but that is not why he died."

The gasp filled the room. "I *knew* you never loved my father!" Helen burst into the room with a cold stare at her mother.

Agnes put a hand to her heart as Beth cried out, "Helen!"

Helen shot a cold glance at Beth, then turned back to her mother.

She continued, words spitting hatred. "As soon as I saw you with that man I knew you loved *him*. It was there for everyone to see…the way you smiled and laughed with him." Helen narrowed her eyes as Annabella swung around. "Why could you not just tell me that all those years ago? Is that the reason you have always been ashamed of me? The reason you never wanted to really claim me as your daughter?"

Annabella gripped her hands at her side. "I never claimed you as my daughter in this town out of respect for my mother! Something you have never had for me. My mother did not want the good people of Rubyville to know that her daughter had a baby outside of marriage."

"So," Helen crossed her arms. "You were a coward instead."

Beth gasped and covered her mouth.

"Helen Barton, that was uncalled for. You know you do not mean that." Agnes addressed her niece with a frown.

Helen switched her cold stare to her aunt. "Yes, I do mean it, Aunt Agnes. My mother was a coward before her parents and this town. Rather than admitting what she had done and claiming me, loving me, she let people think I was someone she found on the streets…just as she had with Beth." Helen's eyes softened as she sought Beth. "I am sorry for hurting you, Beth, but that is what she did."

Beth lowered her head, her shoulders trembling.

Annabella gaped at her daughter. "You have no feelings for anyone, do you? You do not care who you strike out and hurt."

Helen pressed her lips together, her blue eyes turning to liquid. One tear spilled over and tracked down her face as she turned to her mother. "I care, Mama. But I have no one left to claim as my own. Grandpapa, the one person that was proud to call me his granddaughter, is now gone. I have no father and my mother has *never* wanted me."

Annabella rushed to her daughter's side. "I have always loved you, Helen. From the very moment I knew you were growing inside me, I loved you and wanted you. I have always been so sorry that your father never had the chance to love you and see you grow. He would have been *so* proud of you." She brushed Helen's arm. "But you do not understand the ramifications in this world…this *society*, of women having a baby outside of marriage. Good people just do not do that."

"And *if* it happens, you do not share that with others. You should not air your dirty laundry in public." Agnes moved over and took Beth in her arms. "Your mother loves you, Helen, and she has *always* wanted you. Your mother and I took Beth in and raised her as our own daughter because her parents discarded her." Agnes patted Beth on the back. "You have never known true rejection, my girl. You have many lessons to learn in the areas of forgiveness and compassion."

Helen brushed at her red cheek, her eyes flitting over the three women gathered. "I am sure I have many lessons to learn...after all, I am only sixteen. But they will not be learned in Rubyville if I have anything to say about it." She turned to walk from the room and then paused at the arched doorway. "Are we *good people* as you stated, Mama? Or just people, the same as the rest of the town, or even Beth's parents? What defines *good?* In my Bible, we are all just people, sinners saved by grace. God loves us all the same. That is all I asked of you, Mama."

Helen strode from the room, her head held high. She climbed the stairs and the shutting of her bedroom door was heard below.

Chapter Twenty Two

June 1915

"YOU MISSED A WONDERFUL celebration, Annabella." Agnes climbed the steps to the wide porch. She stopped and took a deep breath. "That walk seems to become longer and longer each time. These shoes!" She stuck out one small foot, displaying a pretty, blush pink pump. Several straps crossed the arch of her foot, tiny beads sparkling in the sunlight. "They are *so* very pretty, but they pinch my feet terribly. Perhaps Beth would like them. They would be more fitting on a younger woman, I think." She twisted her foot back and forth, admiring them.

Annabella laughed. "I have never seen you so absorbed in footwear before, Aunt Agnes. You were always lecturing me on the merits of a good, strong walking shoe." She gestured to Agnes's feet as the older woman sat down on the wicker chair next to hers.

Agnes pulled the hat pin from her wide brimmed hat and set the beige and pink confection on the table. She patted her brown hair, streaks of gray liberally interwoven. "I do not know what has come over me. I see that catalog and I cannot help myself."

"Maybe you should work more at the mercantile? Now that Mr. and Mrs. Howard have moved from Rubyville, I could sure use some help." She winked at Agnes. "I will even let you order more shoes."

Agnes threw her head back, and laughed "Well, that makes it all worth it, *of course*." She rested her elbows on the chair arms and clasped her hands in front of her waist. "I thought Beth was helping you at the mercantile?"

"She was, but with summer here, Daniel really needs her help at the hotel. You know how business picks up with the warmer weather." Annabella looked over at Agnes. "So, tell me all about this celebration I missed. I could hear bits of singing and such, every now and then."

"Well, they started off the day with prayer for our men that are fighting in the war."

"That is good. We all need to remember those brave young men. I cannot believe it has been almost a year since it began. We are so protected here in Kansas and it is so very far away. I pray that it ends soon."

Agnes nodded. "And I as well. I can still remember when the Civil War began that April of 1861. I was so young, but it was very frightening, knowing that men were going to die for what they believed. So many families lost loved ones." She looked down at her lap and closed her eyes for a moment.

"I did not mean to stir up hard memories, Aunt Agnes." Annabella reached out and patted her aunt's arm.

Agnes looked up and gave her a half-smile. "It was a lifetime ago, but the scars run deep for so many. I know this war will do the same. It will tear families apart and leave deep wounds, both physically and emotionally." Agnes took a deep breath and continued their previous conversation. "There was a small ceremony for the graduates, as you know. The six of them were so proud of one another." Agnes touched her forehead with her hand. "I almost forgot. There was an announcement that they would be building on to the school over the summer. They need more space for students than what they have in those two large rooms."

Annabella smiled. "I am so happy to hear that. Papa would be pleased."

"Some of the ladies made cake, and there was ice cream and lemonade." Agnes patted her tummy. "That ice cream is delicious. Daniel is thinking of serving it on a regular basis at the restaurant, during the summer months."

"I think that is a wonderful idea. He will need Charles there to keep cranking the freezer."

Agnes laughed. "Yes, that is a good job for a growing boy with a lot of energy." She glanced at Annabella, the smile leaving her face. "I know it would have been difficult to go to the park today and watch the graduation ceremony, but the town needed to see you there, Annabella."

Annabella's eyes swept the front yard and she sighed. "I know, but without Helen there…well, I just could not attend. She should have been with her classmates, rejoicing with them. Not so far away in New York."

"But it is what she wished, Annabella. After that last conversation…" Agnes shook her head. "I just think it was for the best. She is getting a very good education there at The Bennett School for Girls. Many respected families send their daughters there. She enjoys it immensely."

Annabella nodded. "I know, but Millbrook, New York is so far away. She is not even coming home for a visit this summer."

"I understand that you are disappointed, but at least she is staying with my brother's family there in Albany, whenever she has time off from the school. They will take very good care of her." Agnes smiled and bumped Annabella's foot with her own. "Can you imagine how happy your mother would be to know that *her* granddaughter is back where we grew up? She never fully believed Kansas was as civilized as New York."

Annabella laughed and rested her cheek on her hand. "Well, when she graduates, she will be more educated than I ever will be. Rubyville will seem to be smaller and more behind the times than it was when she lived here." Annabella laid her hand in her lap and looked at Agnes. "I fear she will never return to Rubyville."

"Oh…come now. Do not be worrying about things that have not happened. Concentrate on what you do have, and count your blessings. You have many, Annabella."

"So I keep hearing," she smiled. Her face relaxed into a frown once more. "I do need to write Helen and let her know that Misty died. She loved that horse and Misty returned that love. I think she died of a broken heart when Helen left." Annabella turned to Agnes. "Peter told me that Misty just stopped eating. Even when he took her to pasture, she just stood there, her head hanging."

"Maybe, but Misty was also very old. William gave her to you when Helen was barely walking."

"I know, but I don't want to lose anymore horses. My heart cannot take the pain." Annabella covered her mouth with one hand, her elbow resting on the arm circling her waist. "This life is so full of loss. It seems as though it just happens continuously. About the time you take a breath and relax, something new springs up that needs to be dealt with."

"I agree that it seems unrelenting at times. But we do receive moments of refreshment from the burdens. Again, concentrate on those and thank God for them." Agnes's eyes swept over the large front porch and the green yard beyond. "You have always known monetary wealth, Annabella, as have I. We were raised with it, probably took it for granted and even expected it at times. So many people never have that. We have the loss of loved ones and the pain that goes with it. We have the responsibilities of life, but we have never had the burden of wondering where our next meal is coming from, or where we will lay our head at night. So many people in this world are not so fortunate."

Annabella nodded. "God knew He needed to keep you here to help me keep my focus on Him. I would be a very selfish woman without your reminders of all that I have, Aunt Agnes."

Agnes smiled. "It is a good thing that I never married or had children of my own. You have been a full-time occupation, for sure." She leaned back in her chair and closed her eyes. "This warm weather, the sound of the bees, and that delightful breeze are calling for me to take a little nap."

Annabella listened to the light snores from her aunt and smiled. *Thank you, Father, for Your provision. I really do have so much to be thankful for...Aunt Agnes, Martha, Daniel, Beth, and the children. I live in a beautiful part of the country, surrounded by family and friends. I enjoy my work at the mercantile, and taking over from where my parents left off. You have given me so much.* Annabella brushed at the tears trickling down the tiny wrinkles of her face. *Thank you also for my beautiful daughter. I pray that she remembers You in all that she does. Help her to learn everything she can while she is away, and may she use that knowledge for good in her life.*

September 1915

"WHAT A *BEAUTIFUL,* ALMOST autumn day!" Beth closed the screen door to the Barton Mercantile. "Would one of you care to take a

184

walk with me?" She glided to the long wood counter and placed her gloved hands upon the scarred surface.

Agnes turned from stocking cans upon the shelves behind the counter, and brushed her hands upon her white apron. "You are very chipper this morning."

Annabella winked at Agnes. "You would think school had started, but that cannot be, Beth would miss her children too much."

"Oh, you two…you know I love my children…all four of them…but there are days that I *really* enjoy them all being in school. Little Georgie is probably the biggest relief. He is getting better now that he is almost eight…but he still has so much energy. He can get into something faster than I can blink."

Agnes raised a brow. "Just think what his poor teacher is going through. Florence is close to my age. She must be exhausted by the time the day is over," Agnes laughed.

"Well, Georgie loves school, so she must be doing something right. I heard no complaints last year and I know Charles or Dottie would have filled me in if there was anything going on." Beth drummed her fingers on the counter, perusing the shelves behind Annabella and Agnes.

"Ellen has not said anything?" Annabella straightened a bolt of gingham and set it on the stack at the end of the counter.

Beth shook her head. "She and Georgie have always defended one another…maybe because they are the youngest."

"So, there you have it. Ellen and Georgie have sworn Charles and Dottie to secrecy." Agnes slid over a pad of paper and jotted down a list of figures.

Annabella set one hand upon her hip. "That does not explain Florence's silence."

Agnes shrugged. "They obviously have her so worn out that all she can accomplish is to sit behind her desk in a stupor."

Beth laughed. "What am I going to do with the both of you? You are headed to being two crazy old women. What if Florence heard what you just said, Aunt Agnes?"

"I am thinking she would agree with me," Agnes muttered, as she finished her list. She looked at Annabella. "You may go and take a walk with Beth. That way one of us can enjoy this beautiful *almost* autumn day." She glanced at Beth. "What does that mean exactly?"

Beth looked toward the two screen doors at the front of the store. She took a deep breath and closed her eyes. "Smell that on the breeze? The air is cooler and not so muggy. There is a bit of old earth and leaf smell." She opened her blue eyes. "The leaves have not turned yet, but they are getting ready. The days are cooler...even the sun shines differently." She shrugged. "Almost autumn."

Annabella smiled as she took off her apron and hung it on the door to the storage room. "I will have to remember that if I ever decide to wax eloquent on the seasons of the year." She entered the back room and returned, pinning on her blue velvet hat. One peacock feather garnished the close-fitting crown. She adjusted the belt at her waist and smoothed the matching dark-blue skirt.

"I absolutely adore that hat, Mama Bella. That dark shade of blue has always complimented your coloring." Beth walked from the counter, her gaze taking in Annabella's hat.

"I am afraid I do not have much coloring left." Annabella patted the back of her hair. "There is more gray hair than red." She pointed to her cheek. "The freckles seem to endure, however." She turned to Agnes. "You will be fine here, without me?"

Agnes's eyes swept the vacant room. "We have had our usual four customers this morning. I think I can manage until you return."

"It does pick up again later in the morning. I can stay if you would like to take a walk."

Agnes waved a hand at Annabella. "Go on with you, now. You have been anxious to get outside since we opened the store. I know how much you enjoy days like this...and obviously Beth does as well. I may even get a chance to sit for a while and do some reading."

Beth grabbed Annabella's hand. "She is correct...you love days like this. See you after a while, Aunt Agnes." Beth waved as she opened the screen door and pulled Annabella through.

Annabella laughed as they strode down the sidewalk, arm-in-arm. "I feel as though I am being kidnapped" She looked up at the clear, blue sky, white balls of cotton floating lazily. "I do love working at the store, but I really miss being outside, especially on days like this."

"I know you do. Many of my growing up years recalls memories of our walks in St. Louis and then here in Rubyville. Whether it was cold or hot, raining or snowing, not much kept you from being outside." Beth gestured to the white gazebo in the center of the park. "May we sit there for a bit? It will be quiet with all the children in school."

"That sounds fine to me...just as long as we walk around the park at least once. All the standing at the mercantile makes me rather stiff and sore by the end of the day. It feels wonderful to stretch my legs."

They walked across the park, the dark green grass brushing at their skirts. The canopy of leaves floated in the breeze, allowing the sunlight to peek through every now and then. They climbed the stairs to the gazebo and took a seat on the wood bench attached to the walls below the railing.

"I received a letter from Ruth Marlow yesterday." Beth crossed her ankles as she leaned back against the low wall.

"You did? I am so happy to hear that. Aunt Agnes lost touch with them after she moved from St. Louis. She tried writing a few times, but never heard anything in return. She had started to wonder if the family had moved from the area." She looked at Beth, her green eyes sparkling. "You have to tell me everything. They must be in their twenties by now."

Beth laughed. "I will tell you everything I can remember. I should have brought the letter with me." She unbuttoned the light jacket she wore. "It is becoming a bit warm. I had written a few times as well and Ruth always wrote back. But then I did not hear from her for several years. I was so busy with the children that I was not as diligent about corresponding either." She shrugged. "And then I received her letter yesterday."

Annabella frowned. "Is everything alright? I pray their lives have been filled with blessings. They had been through so much, losing their parents at such a young age."

Beth patted Annabella's knee. "Oh, they have been wonderful, both of them. Just very busy growing up and getting married—"

"They are married?" Annabella sat back. "Imagine, little Arthur and Ruth...married."

"Ruth was married back in 1910. She has two children, both boys. The eldest is three and the baby is just nine months old. Arthur married Lillian Beckett in 1913. He is studying and working with his father so that he can pastor their church in a few years."

Annabella frowned. "Why does that name sound familiar?"

Beth smiled. "Lillian Beckett, the little blonde-haired girl in your Sunday school class all those years ago. Arthur was sweet on her. It appears he never changed his mind about that."

Annabella laughed. "Of course…such a pretty little girl. I think half the boys in my class were sweet on her. They do not have any children?"

Beth shook her head. "Not that Ruth mentioned."

"And they are still in the St. Louis area?"

"Ruth and her husband live on a small farm just outside of St. Louis. I believe Arthur and Lillian have a place near the church in St. Louis. Ruth said Arthur and Lillian do much of the same volunteer work that Aunt Agnes and you did."

"I am afraid there will always be a need in that area. It is wonderful that there are still young people willing to do it. You are involved with so many harsh realities of this life." Annabella's eyes looked into the distance.

"Have you heard from Helen?" Beth shrugged out of her jacket and laid it on the bench.

Annabella sighed. "She wrote at the beginning of the term. She sent a postcard with a picture of Halcyon Hall on the front. It is a huge place…originally built as a hotel. She seems very happy there."

"How can you tell, Mama Bella? Whenever she writes me, she chatters about all that she is doing…learning all sorts of things to make her a grand lady. But she never writes of friends…other girls that she is close to."

"I know, Beth. She is never very personal…only writes out of a sense of duty as far as I can tell."

"Well, I think it is utter nonsense that you have not been back there to see her. It was bad enough that she refused you or Aunt Agnes to travel with her when she left home, but to not allow you to visit." Beth shook her head. "I do not understand the girl."

"Well, if this has given her the chance to see the world outside of

Kansas, and she has grown from her experience, it will have all been worth it. For now, if she desires to remain on her own, I will not fight her. She will be nineteen in January…old enough to take care of herself if she wishes." Annabella sat straighter, breathing deeply.

"You are taking all of this much better than I would. It would be like a knife in my heart if one of my children walked out as Helen did, and then refused to see me."

Annabella blinked back the tears. "It *is* a knife in my heart, Beth. But all I can do is give her freedom. I am thankful that she agreed to finish out her school years in Millbrook. I do not know what I would have done if she had just left home. At the school she has rules and guidance, someone to look out for her. I just pray she uses her time there wisely." Annabella gave a half-smile. "Besides, I am in contact with the school every couple of weeks. There is not much I do not know. Aunt Agnes keeps a watch through the family in Albany. I would be there immediately if I had cause for concern."

Beth laughed as she stood. "There is the Mama Bella I know and love. We had better start back if we want to walk around the park first. I told Daniel I would help with the dinner crowd today." She lifted her jacket from the bench and folded it over her arm.

"Is it still that busy at the hotel?" Annabella stood and walked to the stairs.

"It is slowing down. I really do not mind. It gives me a chance to be near Daniel and do some cooking, which I love. I can experiment with some recipes there that I would not try at home."

"Children's tastes in food tend to run fairly plain and simple. A freshly baked loaf of bread and butter always seem to hit the spot."

They left the shade of the park and crossed the street in front of the limestone church. Annabella paused on the sidewalk. "Do you mind if I take a detour to the cemetery? Since I have been working at the mercantile, I do not get there as much as I like. I am sure the weeds have grown up around the headstones."

"That is fine." Beth hugged Annabella and kissed her cheek. "Have a good visit. I know your parents and James are not there, but you just seem closer somehow. Maybe it's the solitude of the cemetery, maybe knowing that their physical body was laid to rest there. It is just different."

Annabella smiled. "That is exactly what I believe. I love you, my dear." Annabella kissed Beth's cheek and waved as she began the long walk to the cemetery at the edge of the woods.

Chapter Twenty Three

ANNABELLA KNELT DOWN IN the grass and pulled at the longer blades surrounding the headstones. "It will be winter again soon, Mama and Papa. I wanted to stop by and make sure everything was tidy before then. I remember you wanting the cemetery to look well-kept, Papa...the grass cut, dead flowers removed. The boy you hired to do that is keeping up with all that you asked of him."

Her eyes swept the small meadow off to the side and in back of the church. Headstones and crosses dotted the shorn grass that flowed into the line of trees behind the church. "I remember you clearing this land while the church was being built. It seemed like such a large area at the time, but each year, more residents of Rubyville make their final resting place here."

Her green eyes sought the two large headstones in front of where she knelt. *William Barton – Founder of Rubyville, Kansas. Born in 1840, died in 1912, united in marriage in May 1862. Lavinia Saunders Barton, born in 1846, died in 1901, beloved wife and mother.* "You both are greatly missed. I hear your laughter, Papa, floating on the air as you drove that automobile you loved so much. Your strong voice blending with Mama's as you sang in church. Mama, your words come to me every time I would like to relax and not wear my shoes, or let my hair down." Annabella smiled. "See, you made an impact on me, even though you thought you had failed."

The small headstone next to Lavinia's brought tears to her eyes. *James Barton, born March 1900, died December 1900. You shared our lives for 8 months; rejoice with the angels, our sweet boy.* "You would be fifteen now, just a couple of years older than Charles. He would have loved to have you here, someone to look up to, and talk with. I do not understand why God took you home to be with Him so soon...but know you were dearly loved by us and you are missed."

She stood and wiped at the tears on her face. "Someday, we will all join you here...Martha, Aunt Agnes, Daniel and Beth, and all of their children and grandchildren. Our physical bodies will be buried, but we will be reunited with all three of you. Thank You for that promise, God, that You have given us in I Thessalonians chapter four, verses thirteen through eighteen. We do comfort one another with these words. We live with hope that we will be together once again." She looked up at the bright, blue sky, hanging above the trees. The white, fluffy puffs calmly stretching and reshaping. A bright-red cardinal sang from a nearby lilac bush, his brown mate tucked inside the green leaves.

May 1925

"AFTER THAT STORM LAST night, I thought for sure we would all be blown away." Martha, her white hair thin and frizzy about her face, rocked back and forth. One wrinkled hand patted the wood arm of the chair. "I surely do appreciate you surprising me with this rocking chair, Annabella. I intend to enjoy many hours in it this summer."

Annabella smiled at the elderly woman. "You are more than welcome, Martha. Maybe it will encourage you to sit more. You should not be on your feet so much at your age."

Martha pulled up the skirt of the black dress she wore and looked at her leather boots, tiny buttons up the front. "These feet have held me up for eighty-one years...and I am praying for a couple more." The wrinkled face turned to her. "Besides, who is going to look after you if old Martha is gone? We are the only two left in this big old house, if you remember."

Annabella nodded, blinking back tears. "I remember, Martha...I remember." She brushed at her eye. "Seems like all I do these days is remember."

Martha sniffed and took a long time sipping her lemonade. She set the glass on the table and looked out over the large, front yard. "I do not want to hear any of that, my girl. If I can go on after losing Lavinia and Agnes, you can too. Those girls were my family ever since..." she sniffed again. "Well, ever since we were practically babies. You and I still have one another and we can look forward to seeing everyone again. In my case, it will be soon, in yours you will have to wait a few more years. God has some more for you to do here. My time is about up."

"Martha, *I* do not want to hear *that*. I cannot face losing you, too." Annabella shook her head and rubbed her temple, before smoothing back the gray hair laced with red. "May we talk about something cheerful?"

Martha laughed, the wrinkles around her eyes swallowing up their sparkle. "I mentioned that storm we had last night…woke me up in the middle of a very nice dream. I guess it is that time of year again."

"Yes, the rain was wonderful. Everything looks so green and new today. But as you said, the wind was terrible. Storms like last night always remind me of the tornado of 1896." Annabella shivered.

Martha smacked her hands on the arm of her chair. "There you go again. You seem to just trail off onto subjects better left in the past." She scooted to the edge of her chair. "I think I am going in to lie down for a bit before I fry that chicken for dinner."

Annabella stood and helped Martha to her feet. "You do not need to make fried chicken, Martha. Just put it in the oven. You will tire yourself out with—"

Martha looked up at Annabella and shook her finger. "Do not be telling me what I can and cannot do. I have a hankering for fried chicken and fried chicken is what *I* am going to make. I have been cooking the meals around this house before you were born, my dear." The stooped figure shuffled to the side porch.

Annabella sighed. "Well then, at least let me help you."

Martha paused and flung over her shoulder, "I just told you I am going to lie down for a bit before I fry the chicken." She shook her head. "You are making me depressed with all your talk of family not here and cities flying about."

She continued walking, her low muttering heard across the porch. "Besides, I *like* to cook by myself. Everyone is always trying to help old Martha. The biggest help is just leaving me alone some days. Gives me time to pray and think about what my Creator has done for me. Better than sitting out here and talking about dead people who are waiting in Heaven for me. I already have an invitation to that big party in the sky, why would I want to think about missing them..." The words were lost as the stooped figure pushed open the screen door to the kitchen.

Annabella rubbed her forehead and looked toward the barn. Peter was puttering around in the large center aisle, moving items back into one of the old horse stalls. *He is probably cleaning again. We must have the best oiled and repaired equipment in the county. I need to sell all that horse tack so he does not have to bother with it anymore. The days of having horses on the Barton property are probably gone.* She started down the stairs of the porch and then paused. *I had better not bother him. If I know Peter, he wants to finish up before dinner.*

She grabbed the railing of the porch and pulled herself back up the stairs. She walked the distance of the house, her brown leather pumps, clicking on the wood boards. The pleated skirt of her dress flared out just below her knees with each step. She crossed one arm around her waist, her elbow resting on it, while her hand toyed with the bow at the deep 'v' of her bodice. She glanced up at the sound of an automobile approaching the house, narrowing her eyes at the black, unfamiliar vehicle.

She uncrossed her arm and smoothed the long waist of her mint-green dress. The finger curls framing her face received attention as well. She craned her neck as she approached the edge of the front porch and laid one slender hand on the white column. "May I help you?" she asked the tall, white-haired man as he shut the front door to the automobile.

He swept off his brown fedora and held the hat at his side as he walked toward the house. "If you are Annabella Barton, you may."

Annabella breathed in and held her breath, placing one hand against her chest. She let it out in a rush and skipped down the stairs. She stopped in front of the brown tweed-suited man, taking in his dark eyes, the wrinkles beside them and the white mustache. She smiled, the corners of her mouth lifting into a grin. "Orin Langworthy, what are you doing here in Rubyville, Kansas?"

His dark eyes twinkled, one white brow arching. "Why, I came to see you, of course."

Annabella threw her arms around his neck and whispered against his ear. "I do not even care if it is proper or not to hug you. It is *so* good to see you again!"

He laughed as he returned the hug, and then pushed away. He held her at arm's length. "Let me take a good look at you." His eyes swept her tall form, from the hair smoothed back into a low bun, to the brown toes of her Mary Jane pumps. "You have not aged a bit, Annabella Barton. You are just as beautiful as you always were."

She pulled her hands away and smiled at him. "And you are a liar, Mr. Langworthy. A sixty-two year old woman cannot possibly look the same as she did in her early twenties."

She looked down at the green grass beneath her feet. "But I thank you for your compliment. It is nice to feel feminine and young again…even if it is not true." She gestured to the porch. "Please come and visit for a while. I am assuming Beth knew you were coming?"

He shook his head as he followed her to the stairs. "No, I did not speak to Beth about my arrival." He reached out and took her hand in his. "I have much to discuss with you, Annabella. Do you have some time, or would it be better if I checked into the hotel first?"

She paused and looked at him, searching his face. "Then you are staying for a couple of days?" Annabella spoke slowly.

He smiled. "Yes, at least that…if it is alright with you, of course."

She gently pulled him up the stairs and led him to the wicker chairs. "I have plenty of time. Martha just went in to lie down and she always naps for a couple of hours."

Orin unbuttoned the three buttons of his suit coat and set his fedora on the table as he waited for her to sit down. He slid into the chair, straightening the collar of his sage-green striped shirt. "So, Martha is still with you?"

Annabella nodded. "Yes, she is doing very well for her age…just tires easily. I pray I am in as good of shape when I reach my eighties."

Orin rested his arms on the chair and looked at Annabella. "Beth wrote me when your aunt passed away. I was very sorry to hear it. Beth said it was pneumonia."

"Yes, it was a very difficult time. Aunt Agnes had never been sick a day in her life that I can recall. She got a bad chest cold and it progressed to pneumonia. She went very quickly." Annabella pressed her lips together and brushed delicately at her nose.

"I would have been here if I was able. My wife, Sarah, was also very sick at the time and I did not want to leave her." Orin cleared his throat and watched his finger slide along the wicker arm of the chair. "She battled cancer for some time. She passed away in June of last year."

Annabella covered the gasp with her hand. "I am so sorry, Orin. Beth did not tell me that."

"I did not share the news with Beth." He pulled on the white cuff of his shirt, twirling the cuff link, as he focused on the line of trees beyond the porch. "I just needed to take some time to adjust to Sarah being gone. She had been such a support and help to me for so many years. My life seemed fairly hopeless for awhile. I guess I just needed to learn how to live again, without her." He looked at Annabella. "We were married almost twenty-three years. She was a wonderful wife and mother…much more than I ever deserved."

"You have had a very difficult year, then." Annabella reached out and covered his arm with her hand. "How are your children doing with the loss of their mother? They must be a great comfort to you."

He smiled. "Yes, they are. Beatrice is twenty-two and has been married for three months. Mark is twenty and traveling Europe."

"Europe, what an exciting opportunity! Has he been gone long?"

"He left right after Beatrice's wedding and has plans to be gone a year or more." He covered the hand that rested on his arm. "So, you can see, I am very alone in this world." The dark eyes swept her face.

Annabella pulled her hand away and sat back in her chair. She clasped her hands in her lap. Her eyes rested on the black automobile in the driveway. "That is beautiful. I was wondering what make it was. I do not think I have seen anything with those wings on the hood. It looks very different than Aunt Agnes's model-T Ford."

Orin smiled. "So your aunt had a 'Tin Lizzie'?"

Annabella frowned. "It is a very nice mode of transportation, and I still use it." She gestured to the black machine. "It is not as elegant as that, but Aunt Agnes was very pleased with it."

"I do not know why I should be surprised that your aunt owned a vehicle. She was a very modern woman." He raised a brow. "So, you know how to drive?"

"Well, of course I do, Orin. I have been driving for many years now. Papa taught both Aunt Agnes and me when he purchased his first automobile back in 1907."

Orin whistled. "That sounds just like your father. He was always one step ahead of the rest of the world when it came to new inventions, and new ways of doing things." He pointed to the automobile. "That is a 1924 Chrysler Six, Model 70. That means—"

"*That* means it can travel up to seventy miles per hour." She shook her head. "I cannot even imagine." She glanced at him. "You seem surprised that I know the answer to that. I have an interest in automobiles, Aunt Agnes did as well. I know it is a strange past time for a woman, but I find them fascinating. Every year, they seem to be getting better and better. Papa knew they would replace the horse, and I really think he was correct."

"In the bigger cities, they pretty much have." Orin rubbed his chin. "Well, you have done it again, Annabella. You have taken the wind right out of my sails."

"And why is that?"

He sat forward in his chair. "I came here today, in the middle of my journey, to ask you to be a part of it. I am excited about it and I was hoping you would be free to share in it with me. I had no idea you would be so prepared to partake of it."

Annabella frowned. "Your journey?" She slumped back in her chair. "I am very confused, Orin. You are talking in riddles, and I cannot make any sense of them."

"I purchased that automobile shortly after Sarah passed away. I sold our home in Pennsylvania, said my good-byes to the children and I started driving. I have seen so much of this country by train. Now I want to take it all in slowly, driving from the east coast to the west coast."

"You can do that now?" Annabella asked, her eyes lighting up.

He chuckled. "Of course you can. If you are interested in

automobiles, you should have heard about it by now. They have been talking about it for years."

"*Talking* about it and actually *doing* it are two different things, Orin." She looked at him. "So you have been driving all this time?"

He nodded. "Yes, for a couple of months now. I have been just taking my time...enjoying the scenery, visiting new places, meeting people." He laughed. "The roads are not in the best of condition in a lot of places, so that does slow you down a bit...but I am not in a hurry." He laughed again and smoothed the white mustache. "I would like to reach the west coast before I turn seventy. I may be pushing that."

Annabella's eyes sought the vehicle once again. "So, everyday, you just get in and drive down this road—"

"It is called the National Old Trails Road, by the way." Orin smiled at her.

Annabella looked heavenward and sighed. "Yes, I have read about it. That and the Lincoln Highway have been some time in the making, if I remember correctly. *So*...everyday, you just get in and drive down this road...and today you ended up here in Rubyville?"

He laughed. "Something like that. I do take little detours now and then. I went through Osage City yesterday and today I arrived here, by choice. The next stop will be Council Grove."

Annabella pressed her hands together. "That does sound exciting. To think, just get in your automobile and drive until you want to stop for the night. No worries, just lots of time to take in the scenery and see new places. What fun!" Annabella's eyes sparkled as she looked at Orin.

He smiled at her. "I knew you would understand. But it is not all beautiful, sunny skies and no worries. The traveling can be rather rough in some areas. A rainy day rather dampens the spirit after awhile. I have gone through tires and have had to make repairs along the road. But yes, I have enjoyed it immensely."

Annabella waved a hand at him. "Even carriages and wagons broke down. Horses would throw a shoe or become sick. Nothing is perfect."

Orin nodded, "That is true. Any kind of travel is not without grievance." He brushed away a ladybug from his trousers and continued. "So, my plan when I first started out was just as you described. But as the days passed and then the weeks, I was becoming a little lonely. I was thinking of someone that I would love to share the trip with. This person would have to be someone that I enjoyed talking to, someone that challenged me, and kept life interesting. Before long, I started thinking of you, Annabella." He reached into the inside pocket of his suit coat and pulled out a tintype. He passed it to Annabella. "I would place it on the seat beside me, and think of things you would say. I could picture your face and smile, with each situation that came up."

Annabella looked down at her much younger likeness. "I gave this to you back in 1886…just before we were to be married." She looked up at him. "You have kept this all these years?"

"It was all I had of you." His dark eyes captured hers. "I have always missed you, Annabella."

"Why did you come to Rubyville, Orin?" The words hung heavy in the silence.

"I came because I want you to continue the journey with me, Annabella. I want you to share in it. It will not be easy, there will be many detours, and it will take a long time. But if I am with you, it will not matter how long it takes." His eyes took in her hair, the green eyes, and the rose-colored lips. "I want you to come with me."

Annabella stood and walked to the railing, gripping it with both hands. "Orin, I would love to take a journey such as that. It sounds exciting and challenging…but…"

Orin slid from his chair and walked up behind her. He whispered against her ear, "But what?"

She looked over her shoulder at him. "We cannot travel alone, you and me, across the country. It is not proper. I cannot believe you came here to ask me such a thing, Orin Langworthy." She turned and crossed her arms. "No, I cannot do it. I would not be able to sleep at night with my mother's words pounding in my head about how wrong I was."

He chuckled and placed his hands on her upper arms, letting them slide to her elbows. "Did you ever become the proper young lady your mother wanted you to be, Miss Annabella Barton?"

Annabella trembled. "I tried hard enough…for many years. But now

I do understand that I cannot do anything under my own strength and willpower. I have become strong and more content with God's guidance, but I have a long way to go yet." She trembled again. "You should not be making me feel the things I am feeling Orin Langworthy."

"And what are these *things* you are speaking of?" Orin caressed her elbows.

"When you are sixty-two years old, wrinkled and gray-headed, you should not feel all warm and tingly inside like a school girl." Annabella sighed and shrugged away from Orin.

"Why not?" Orin leaned against the tall, white column of the porch, and slid his hand into his trouser pocket. "Who says that as you age you cannot have romantic feelings for someone? Where is the rule that states that you cannot feel your heart race at the sound of their voice, or the touch of their hand?"

"All those emotions are for the young." Annabella crossed her arms and stared at him. "So…back to your offer of the journey in your automobile." She glanced at it once again and sighed. "I would love to take such a trip as that, but I will not, *cannot* do it with you. I have struggled with my reputation in this town for years; I do not need to heap more coals upon my head."

"Why would it concern the good citizens of Rubyville if you took an automobile trip with your husband?" Orin's eyes swept the length of her. "It certainly would not be an option for us to travel alone, if we were not married."

Annabella opened her mouth and then closed it, staring at him. "Are you saying we should get married?"

He smiled, the white mustache lifting at the corners. "Yes, I am! I have asked you enough over the past forty years." He chuckled. "I do not know about you, but I do not have another forty to wait." He shrugged. "I rather enjoyed being married and I want to experience it with you…if you will have me, of course."

Annabella put a hand to her chest and walked to the chair. She sat down on the edge of the chair, her elbows upon her knees. "What about your children? What if they do not want you to marry again…or they do not like me? Are you sure you are ready to be married? You said Sarah has only been gone a year. Helen will be—"

Orin knelt before Annabella and took her hands. "Shhh, my dear." He pressed a kiss to her fingers. "My family has always known that we were to be married. Sarah knew that I loved you. Before she died, she encouraged me to find you again. She did not want me to be alone in my old age, and my children do not as well."

"Sarah knew that you loved me?" Annabella searched Orin's eyes. "That was a cruel thing to tell her."

"Sarah and I were always truthful with one another. She knew that I would love her and care for her and the children, putting them first in my life...which I did." Orin's eyes filled with tears. "But she loved me enough, to send me back to you, and my children want me to be happy as well."

Annabella turned from the sadness in Orin's eyes. "I wish I could say the same for Helen. I fear she will be very upset by all of this. You obviously did a much better job of raising your children than I did with Helen."

"I would not say that. You raised Beth as well and she is a wonderful wife and mother. She has a very caring and loving heart." He smiled. "I think she would be happy for us."

Annabella smiled. "Yes, she would be."

Orin grinned and pressed a kiss to her hand once more. "So, while I am kneeling here, please give me an answer, Annabella Barton. Will you marry me, and travel this fine country of ours from coast-to-coast?"

Annabella smiled down at the earnest look on Orin's face and laughed. "Kansas is not exactly on a coast. We are about as close as you can get to the middle."

Orin dropped his head and shook it. He looked up at her once again, his dark eyes shining. "You do make me feel alive and young, Annabella Barton. That road stretches out in both directions. If you would like, we can drive back to the east coast and begin again...just as long as I am with you." He held up one finger. "There is one condition though."

Annabella smiled, her green eyes dancing. "And what might that be?"

"If you say *yes*, we are married the second we are able...none of this preparing for a wedding ceremony six months from now. Neither of us has that kind of time to waste. I also want someone with you at all times, making sure that nothing happens until we are husband and wife."

"Actually, those are *two* conditions." She held up as many fingers. "I absolutely agree with the first condition. I will marry you this afternoon, if possible, after we have fried chicken for dinner. Martha really had her heart set on it. And I do agree that I should not be left alone. Trouble just seems to find me."

Orin gripped her hands and grinned up at her, his white teeth standing out against his tanned face. "Is this *really* going to happen for us?"

Annabella nodded and flung her arms around his neck. "I love you so very much, Orin Langworthy."

Orin kissed her cheek and breathed deeply of her scent. "And I love you, my dearest Annabella. I have returned to my place of refuge, my strength, and desire. I pray we have many happy years together."

A Note From the Author

It was a joy for me to write this book, the second in the *Rubyville* series. I loved going back in time and continuing with Annabella Barton's story. She is such a strong, opinionated woman of her generation, struggling with her place in society, just as many women do.

Of course *A Place of Refuge* is fiction. But even fiction is anchored in some truths. I have always loved history, clothing styles through the centuries, and cars. (Yes, I even took a class in high school on how to rebuild an engine!) It was so much fun to research each of these areas to be as accurate as possible in my story. Thank you to the World Wide Web for much of my research. I read *so* many articles, blogs, newspapers, etc. to gain an understanding, that to list each one here would be a book in itself! I want to say a big thank-you for all those that share their information and make it available through the internet. It has been a tremendous help to me.

If you would like to learn more of any of those areas I listed above, just type in what you are looking for. I found loads of information for each decade of clothing styles I used in my story. Car experts share online, and again, there is tons of interesting things to learn about the automobile's history. If you type in the cars I named, you can see actual pictures of them, if you are interested. And yes, there really was a very damaging tornado that hit the city of St. Louis on May 27, 1896. Again, you can find newspaper articles and pictures of this catastrophe.

Thank you for reading, *Rubyville: A Place of Refuge*. I hope you enjoyed it *almost* as much as I did writing it. And as always, I *love* hearing from my readers!

About the Author

Deborah Ann Dykeman has been married for thirty-one years and has five fantastic children. At the last count, she had three wonderful sons-in-law and three grandchildren, with another on the way. She has homeschooled her children, taught Sunday school, been an AWANA director, and worked as a CNA. Her love of history has been the inspiration for 'Rubyville'. Many old towns lay silent and abandoned across the state of Kansas. Buildings stand, reflecting what they once were. The desire to remember these towns and the people that were a part of them is at the heart of this book. Deborah resides in the state of Kansas in the beautiful Flint Hills region. Her first book, *To Thee I'm Wed*, was published in 2015.

Rubyville: A Place of Refuge is the second in the Rubyville series.

Connect with Me:

Like my Facebook page:
http://www.facebook.com/deborahanndykeman

Subscribe to my blog:
http://deborahanndykeman.com

THE COMPLETE
Rubyville
SERIES
BY DEBORAH ANN DYKEMAN

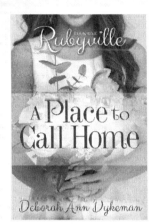

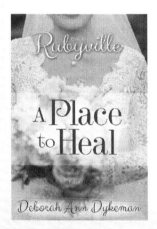

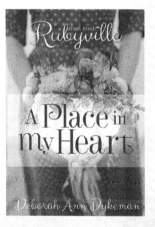

Books available on www.Amazon.com

The entire series available this fall.

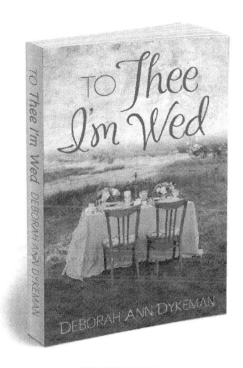

Also by DEBORAH ANN DYKEMAN

Jason and Kathy Miller are brimming with hope and excitement for their future together as husband and wife on their wedding day in June of 1983.

Twenty years later life isn't so carefree anymore. Three children, several pounds, and graying hair have dampened enthusiasm, and Kathy is feeling it. Caring for a home, husband, and teenagers isn't always as fulfilling as a woman would want it to be . . . and that's where problems begin for the Millers.

Kathy now travels a road she would never have considered walking as a young, exuberant bride. Jason struggles along, clearing a path through the thorns that have become their marriage. Will a new baby repair all the damage done or shred the last ties binding them together?

Available on www.Amazon.com

Made in the USA
Charleston, SC
04 October 2016